Advance Praise for
Real Talk, 2e

You're not going to believe this ... or maybe you will. Some people are still using the same approach to making presentations as they did prior to the pandemic. Times have changed! Audiences have changed! And what people want has changed, too. They don't want presenters to show up and throw up information. They want an experience! They want to be transformed! They want to feel, see, and hear (and I'm not talking volume) what you're saying! And they want to be engaged! And if you want the keys to doing that, you have to read Real Talk. *Remember, just because you taught it doesn't mean they caught it. Just because it was said doesn't mean it stayed in their head.* Real Talk *teaches you how to connect with heads and with hearts. It teaches you how to get out of your own way. It helps you to become a lights-out speaker, in-person and from a distance. Bridgett McGowen, a phenomenal speaker, trainer, and coach in her own right, takes you on an amazing, practical, amiable journey to taking your presentations beyond the next level. And she does it in a very straightforward way. Trust me—and I've been speaking professionally for over 35 years—this book is so needed now. Your audiences will thank you for investing in it.*

—Dr. James Smith, Jr.
President & CEO, Dr. James Smith Jr.
Author, Speaker, Visionary, and Consultant

If you are looking for a breakthrough in your public speaking, look no further than Bridgett McGowen's new edition of Real Talk. *Her content is both smart and witty, delivered in a refreshingly conversational style. I've had the privilege of working with Bridgett in-person and she is a FIREBALL of energy. The book managed to surpass my expectations displaying an ability to authentically capture her real-life sizzle while masterfully shifting the focus away from herself to you, the reader. Her honest presentation of the challenges that we speakers face is sobering, but she immediately encourages you with a step-by-step blueprint to finding a solution that fits your speaking style. In* Real Talk, *Bridgett achieves the impossible for any writer, leaving no stone unturned while being succinct with her solutions. Bridgett is living proof of the strategies she shares. I am confident you will walk away more centered, poised, and equipped to navigate any curve balls that come your way on stage, helping you achieve public speaking success.*

—DanRam
Event MC/Moderator, 5x TEDx Speaker,
and Public Speaking Coach

Being able to control your room is a service to your audience. Bridgett McGowen has done it again. She teaches power techniques any exceptional presenter must use with a no-nonsense approach on how to keep your audience front and center. Her humor and end of story statements will keep you smiling while learning because they are not up for discussion. For example:

"Use a mic. Period." As a speaking expert, I can tell you making your room clear, focused, and flowing does not happen by chance. This book is a must-read every professional should have on their bookshelf!

—Monique Russell
Global Communications Expert

Are you interested in looking, sounding, and feeling like a master behind the microphone? Bridgett McGowen has got you covered. Based on her profound knowledge as a presentation expert and her own experience as a professional speaker, she offers immediately applicable, useful, and practical advice in her latest book, Real Talk. *Whether you're presenting online at webinars or face-to-face, this book features dozens of techniques that will help you design, facilitate, and present in a way that keeps your audiences engaged and catapults your performance and self-esteem to new heights. You should get a copy as soon as possible if you want to improve your communication and presentation skills to leave an impactful first and lasting impression.*

—Sylvie di Giusto, CSP
International Keynote Speaker about First and
Lasting Impressions in Sales, Customer Service, and Leadership

Every time you give a speech, a pitch, or address a company meeting, you're giving a presentation. This book equips you with the skills necessary to be professional, persuasive, and powerful. The author, a successful professional speaker herself, shares tips learned from experience. As a consultant in the speaking industry, I've read lots of books on this subject. I highly recommend Bridgett's book as a must-read!

—Lois Creamer
Owner, Book More Business

Real Talk

SECOND EDITION

Sylvie,
What can I say?! Your
praise for Real Talk, 2e is
classy and powerful — just
like you! Thank you so very
much. Keep sizzling!

BZMcHawk

Real Talk

What Other Experts Won't Tell
You About How to Make
Presentations That Sizzle

SECOND EDITION

BRIDGETT McGOWEN

BMcTALKS Press
4980 South Alma School Road
Suite 2-493
Chandler, Arizona 85248

SECOND EDITION

Library of Congress Control Number: 2022913978

ISBN: 978-1-953315-23-6

Interior design by Medlar Publishing Solutions Pvt Ltd., India.

Cover design by BMcTALKS Press.

Printed in the United States of America.

Notice to Booksellers: This book is distributed by IngramSpark and retails for $29.99 USD.

DEDICATION

For Aaron and Parker

FOREWORD

Before you make another presentation, you must read this book!

Highly effective speaking is not a skill that's achieved overnight; but when it *is* achieved, you feel the difference. And so does your audience. You feel invincible. You feel unshakable. You feel unstoppable. *Real Talk, 2e* gets you there.

My love for taking to the stage formed during my childhood when, as a young boy, I would watch my father facilitate seemingly perfect sales presentations. With nothing but the words coming out of his mouth, my dad was able to move people to action.

I was in awe!

To know I could perfect the art of talking and do the same was astoundingly remarkable to me and totally captivating! And to think that little boy from Atlanta, Georgia would go on to land a direct sales position where I was surrounded by, traveling with, and prospecting alongside the likes of Zig Ziglar; Dr. Napoleon Hill; J. Douglas Edwards; Fred Herman; Og Mandino; James H. Rucker, Jr.; and far too many other giants in the industry to name.

I've appeared on 5,000+ stages in front of audiences totaling more than 2.5 million people all around the globe, and I introduced the sales industry to *The Closers* series. It includes world-famous books, audio programs, newsletters, podcasts, and seminars and is the most popular and most powerful sales training material ever produced.

And *Real Talk, 2e* is packed with a power of a different kind. Bridgett is one of the most passionate professional speakers I've ever watched. She and I connected over a love for speaking—not just speaking but intentional, dynamic, carefully choreographed speaking. Our first meeting was on her podcast, *Own the Microphone,* and it was clear from the start that she fully believes anyone—with the right tools—can do the same. We laughed over what we know now and what we wish we'd know then and commiserated over missteps we've personally experienced and how we would have loved some do-overs. And we related time and time again about what makes for an effective, mind-blowing presentation.

For more than twenty years, Bridgett has been making presentations that make audiences go "Wow!" She knows the secret sauce. She knows what it takes on-stage and, most importantly, off-stage to give a performance that's red-hot!

In *Real Talk, 2e,* you do not get the typical recommendations we've all seen over the years that suggest how to give a presentation. This book breaks down presentation preparation and delivery in a way that is real, that is genuine, that is compelling, that is easy to understand, and that makes you want to try every strategy. In these pages, you will see challenges faced by presenters everyday that are tackled with solid solutions. You will get answers to questions you've always wondered about. You will walk away knowing what you've never been told before—approaches to speaking you may have never realized were necessary to be a class act whenever you have a presentation.

Real Talk, 2e details real situations that real speakers experience and guides you through how to expertly handle anything that comes your way as a speaker. Novice speakers will be fired-up and ready to get on any stage, seasoned professionals will find gems that position them to further sharpen their craft, and everyone will get a good laugh or two from Bridgett's subtle insertions of her unique personality and light-hearted humor.

Bridgett owns the presentation skills space. She can watch anyone present for five minutes max and tell you exactly what's working, what's not working, and how to improve. She doesn't sugar-coat anything, and she gives you strategies that not only work but that are the precise strategies she uses herself.

Her presentations are sought after by leading organizations, and her performances consistently deliver. It doesn't matter if it's a webinar, a keynote, a commencement address, a breakout, a workshop, a training—it doesn't matter—she arrives on the scene, gives nothing less than 100 percent, and insists on anyone else who *thinks* about getting on a stage to do the same. With what she provides you in the pages that follow, you, too, will find yourself demanding no less of yourself than your absolute best. With *Real Talk, 2e*, your presentations can only get better, your confidence can only get stronger, and the transformations you bring your audiences can only get bigger.

Before you make another presentation, read this book! You will wish you could go back and redo every single one you've already delivered. But the good news is, with what you learn in *Real Talk, 2e*, all your future presentations will be of the caliber and dynamism you have always been destined to deliver!

All the best!

Ben Gay, III
Author of *The Closers*
bfg3@directcon.net

PREFACE

If you purchased the first edition of *Real Talk*, then I thank you for coming back for more. If this is your first experience with *Real Talk*, then get ready because this will be the best presentation skills book you will ever read. Guaranteed.

But do not just read this book. Study it. Add sticky notes and flags. Bend the edges of pages to remind you of important material. Apply the strategies to your preparation, your practice, and your presentations. When a strategy works, keep doing it. If a strategy isn't a good fit for you, then feel confident and feel free to put it to the side.

This book provides the missing link between what you learned in public speaking courses and what actually happens on the stage, demystifying what the best speakers do. It gives you the answers to the most pressing questions I've received over the years from audiences of professionals yearning to know how to make the best presentations possible.

And just as was the case with the first edition of *Real Talk*, which won a 2020 Best Indie Book Award, if you are looking for quick fixes or the promise of instant changes in your speaking, then this is not the book for you. If you want a book loaded with empirical data, research, statistics, and case studies, this is still not it.

But …

If you want no-nonsense, practical, ready-to-use advice and strategies that are based on my work as an award-winning international professional speaker—work that I've been performing since 2001 with the successful design and facilitation of hundreds of webinars and face-to-face presentations in the form of keynotes, breakout sessions, workshops, trainings, and more to thousands of people positioned all around the globe, presentations that are consistently met with enthusiastic applause and rave reviews—then this is the book for you.

If you want to know what to do but also what *not* do, then you are in the right place.

If you want to skip the suggestions you've read, heard, and tried that simply do not work and you want to know how to make presentations that your audiences love and that you are proud to deliver, then I've got you covered.

Everything I provide in these pages is precisely what I do in my own presentations. So, if you want real talk that leads to presentations that sizzle, then read on, my friend. Read on.

Bridgett McGowen
Chandler, Arizona
October 2022

ACKNOWLEDGMENT

Simone, in the summer of 2022, you lit the fire under me while in Puerto Rico, and I took the flame and ran with it. Thank you for always pushing me to do better, to be better, to be more. Love you always and forever.

TABLE OF CONTENTS

Chapter 1

Build Your Confidence and Crush the Jitters . . . 1

Chapter 2

Establish Your Credibility 51

Chapter 3

Give Everyone a Reason to Listen to You 83

Chapter 4

Deliver Absolutely Flawless Presentations . . . 145

Chapter 5

Ensure You Always Sizzle **215**

NEW TO THIS EDITION

EXPANDED AND REVAMPED CONTENT

1. Why You Get Nervous Before a Presentation and the Expert Practice Strategy Guaranteed to Change That

2. 8 Secrets to Adjust Your Use of "Uh," "Um," and Other Filler Words

3. The Way You Have Been Introducing Yourself to Audiences is All Wrong

4. The Body Language That's Required to Own the Room

5. Does Your Look Match Your Message?

6. No Impressive Bio or Background? No Problem!

7. How You Must View Yourself as a Presenter This Moment Forward

8. The Huge Mistake Presenters Make and How to Avoid It

9. The One and Only Way to Every Start Your Presentation

Chapter 1

BUILD YOUR CONFIDENCE AND CRUSH THE JITTERS

Chapter 1

BUILD YOUR CONFIDENCE AND CRUSH THE JITTERS

Practicing in front of a mirror does not work.

Practicing for friends and family is an exercise in futility as well. (I'll tell you why later. For now, please just stop doing it, okay? You're wasting everyone's time.)

Envisioning a naked audience or finding a focal point on the back wall and training your eyes on it doesn't work nor does it make any sense either—not if you want to look like a pro.

Taking deep breaths and meditating or listening to your favorite jam before stepping on the stage is not the trick. (Let me be clear. You can meditate and rock out to music, but to ensure you have a great performance, you need to do *far* more than that and *well* before your presentation.)

When you engage in any of these practices and little else, you still have the jitters, and the confidence is not where you want it to be.

But why?!

These are strategies other experts have told you to attempt. So, why aren't they working?

They don't work because, on their own, the acts are inadequate. They are not enough to prepare you to shake the jitters and to wow the crowd. Much work must be done beforehand—before you take the deep breaths, before you listen to your favorite beats, before you get on the stage. Building your confidence takes time and, above all, it takes conscious and intentional effort.

You are about to know how to ...

- respect and embrace the important role that jitters play in getting you ready for your presentation
- recognize why it's highly likely your current methods of practicing are giving you a false sense of confidence
- institute easy tactics on a daily basis that will have you presentation-ready at a moment's notice

- instantly feel and sound more confident by identifying and eliminating words you currently use that diminish your credibility and simultaneously show your nervousness

- convey confidence at the start of your presentation with the use of two very specific words

- check the rate at which you speak to ensure your speed is appropriate so you do not feel or sound nervous

- use body language practices to immediately feel more powerful and less anxious

THE JITTERS START WITH THE WAY YOU PRACTICE AND THE WAY YOU PRACTICE IS ALL WRONG

How you practice is how you will perform. If you have not put confidence behind your practice, the confidence will not show up for your performance.

> ### REAL TALK PRINCIPLE
> The key to doing anything well is repetition, but you cannot repeat ineffective habits and expect effective returns.

If you have you ever practiced a presentation in front of a mirror or if you've practiced before a mock audience of supportive friends, family, or colleagues, I know it didn't hit the mark, and I wasn't even there *with* you. When you got on stage, the jitters were still there. That's because you did a great job with repetition but while using not-so-great strategies.

This kind of practice is all wrong, and your efforts to diminish the jitters do not work because you are isolating your practice for only when you need to prepare for a presentation as opposed to engaging in effective communication practices on a daily basis. And it does not work because what you see in the mirror is not a true representation of who you are on-stage and what your audience will see. It also does not work because your audience of friends, family, and colleagues are familiar faces whom you love (or like), and none of these people have the heart or the expertise to tell you that you are doing a poor job. Allow me to repeat that. Rehearsing in front of people who are not presentation skills experts puts you in front of people who do not have the HEART to tell you that your presentation is ineffective and/or they do not have the EXPERTISE to tell you where you are going wrong nor how to improve. And even if they *do* tell you it needs work, they do not know *what* to tell you to do to fix your presentation. So, rehearsing in front of friends is really a waste.

Additionally, I need you to *really* think about this. If you practice only when it's show time, then you are not really doing everything you can to improve—to show up and show out. You are not ensuring that you operate at peak performance levels when it matters. And, if part of your practice involves you listening to a person who will only give sugar-coated, misguided, or uninformed feedback, then you are failing yourself. The good news is this can be turned around.

If you want to get rid of the jitters … if you want to be at peak performance … if you want audience buy-in … then you must shift your mind to think of practice in a new way. This means you put in the necessary presentation skills work every single day. You do not wait until it is time to make a presentation to work on your speaking skills.

Every single time you speak, no matter the person you are addressing or for how long you are speaking—I'm talking about on the phone, at the grocery store, in the bank, with your child's teacher—it does not matter—every single time you open your mouth, speak as if you are giving a presentation.

REAL TALK PRINCIPLE

Do not wait until it is time to make a presentation to pay attention to the way you speak.

Make eye contact with your listener. Speak clearly, articulating every syllable. Speak as if you are being critiqued because, well, you are! People form an impression of you—good, bad, fairly, or unfairly—within seven seconds of seeing you or within the first 11 words that come out of your mouth—they do!—so speak with conviction. Speak to ensure your message is heard and understood. Do this every day. Make everything you say a presentation. That way, when you get on stage to present, you already know how to sound confident when you speak. You sound like your natural self. You do not feel as though you are putting on an act. Rather, you are giving your real self in a true, authentic way.

Furthermore, when you extend your practice beyond the days leading up to your performance, it positions you to be seen as a confident being. Now let me be clear: you still must consciously practice your presentations. Practice each presentation full-out a minimum of three times before every performance.[1]

But for every day when you are not on a stage, at a minimum, engage in all the following:

- clearly articulate your message

- speak loudly enough so you are heard

- hold your head up and keep shoulders back regardless of whether you are standing, sitting, or walking

- consistently use your ideal speaking voice[2]

- make eye contact

- smile

I cover more about the power of the smile and what it demonstrates to the world in *Show Up and Show Out: 52 Communication Habits to Make You Even More Unforgettable.*

When you change the frequency with which you practice and you put in the work on a daily basis with your speaking skills, the anxiety subsides. The nervousness remains at bay. You are no longer bound by the fears of falling short or the worries of making a misstep with your words. You are sure of your words. You are positive and feel strongly about your message. And even if you *do* have a hiccup, you are not completely derailed by it.[3] When you focus on your words and speaking with confidence every day—not just when you have to give a formal presentation on a mic—it becomes far, far easier to get in front of any audience. It does. You are able to give your message with utmost confidence—a confidence that says, "I dare you to tell me I do not know what I'm doing up here!"

And here's my why behind this: I can remember how, as a child, before getting on the avocado green rotary phone (with the shag carpet to match) to dial up a friend and ask a simple question, I would practice down to the letter what I would say. And to this day, when people ask what I do for a living, I tell them I'm a professional speaker, and they immediately respond with "Oh! That makes sense that you're a speaker. That's why you sound like that," I want to tell them that what they hear—that confidence—is not because I'm a professional speaker. I don't sound confident because I'm a professional speaker. It's the other way around—I became a professional speaker because I already sounded confident. I consistently put in the work no matter what I say, and it's because of that regular *work* that I am a professional speaker. On the cool, because I (and so many others) like the sound, feel, and look of confidence, there's no doubt that I'd sound the exact same way even if I *wasn't* a professional speaker.

Don't wait until gametime to put in the work; make focusing on your speaking skills a daily activity.

---

[1] For details on exactly how to practice your presentation full-out, see "Why You Get Nervous Before a Presentation and the Expert Practice Strategy Guaranteed to Change That" in chapter 1.

[2] See "Make This One Change to Sound Confident Every Single Time You Speak" in chapter 1.

[3] For how to handle a misstep, see "What to Do if You Experience a Misstep in the Middle of Your Presentation" in chapter 5.

WHY YOU GET NERVOUS BEFORE A PRESENTATION AND THE EXPERT PRACTICE STRATEGY GUARANTEED TO CHANGE THAT

If you do not feel nervous before a presentation, then this could signal problems ahead. You read that correctly. You *want* to experience nervousness before you present but not to the point where you are overcome by it. When you do, it means you care about giving the audience a meaningful experience. You care about not just talking and checking the boxes on the information you want to deliver. The nerves mean you are 100 percent focused on having a successful performance. However, if you do not have nerves before your presentation, then, well … brace yourself. It is a sure sign you are phoning it in, winging it, or flying by the seat of your pants. Even the most polished of professional speakers will have nerves—not because they are afraid they will not do well but because they want to ensure they do *indeed* do well.

Anyone who wants to bring value to the audience, who wants to bring about a transformation for listeners, who wants to make a difference, who wants to deliver and not talk simply for the sake of talking will experience nervousness. I am not suggesting you should be sweating bullets, knocking at the knees, and looking a complete mess before it is showtime. I *am* suggesting that you should have a slight knot in your stomach or a tiny pull at your heart that says "This has to be a winner. This must go off without a hitch. I am obligated to do a good job so my audience walks away with value."

So, again, nerves making an appearance is a situation you do not necessarily want to eradicate. Nervousness, though, becomes a challenge when it gets in the way of your performance. As such, you want to keep the nerves while learning how to manage them. First, you must understand why the nerves make an appearance before you can work to better manage them. There are two main reasons nerves show up before your presentation.

The first reason nerves show up is because we hope that everyone will like what we say. We are so genuinely worried about whether the audience will like our presentation that we start second-guessing ourselves. "Should I say this? Should I say that? Should I start with a joke?[1] Should I not? What if they don't like me?"

Concern over whether the audience will like us or our presentations happens because we are social beings and we want to be liked—even loved or revered. When we are put into a situation where there is a possibility we will be challenged; where we may not be liked for our ideas, research, or beliefs; or where there is a possibility the audience is not as passionate about our content as are we, nervousness arises. And this nervousness is heightened if we have anxiety to go along with it, which is the physical response to the nerves or the stress—the sweaty palms, the racing heart, the butterflies in the stomach.

A second reason that nerves show up is because you have not spoken the words before. You have engaged in ineffective practice, and the fear is there because you have not heard what you are going to say! If you have not yet heard the words you plan to speak, then you are truly blindly going into your presentation, and that is down-right scary. You know that scene in the movie where the guy buys the ring and wants to pop the question. He does not just *think* about the question. He verbalizes the question. Once. Twice. Over. And over. And over again. So, when he finally says it when it's go time, it's not a foreign utterance. He feels confident.

If the extent of your practice is to mentally go through your presentation, then that is a huge problem. You have no idea how the words will sound, what gestures you will make, nor what facial expressions will accompany each sentence. That kind of practice is wholly ineffective. Additionally, that practicing in the mirror jazz—that doesn't work either. That does not help you get rid of the jitters, and here's why:

When you practice in front of the mirror, you are practicing for the reflection, not for the real thing. You're checking out what you *think* the audience will see. You are putting on a show that may be more artificial than it is authentic. When in front of a mirror, you are not your natural self. Instead, you are what you would like for the people to see. You suck in the gut, turn just so, and try to get the right pose. When you practice, you need to be more natural, more yourself. You need to gesture as you do when you are simply being yourself and speaking as you ordinarily do on a daily basis. To engage in practice that fosters this, practice anywhere but in front of a mirror.

So, to get over the nerves—or to better control them—to not worry about whether the audience will love what you say, and to feel confident in your message, here are the two big changes you must make that will diminish all of that:

First, immediately give your audience a reason to lean in and listen. The first words out of your mouth set the tone for your presentation. They do. Just as on the first day of class, you assess the teacher to determine if this is someone you can railroad, if it's someone you will like, or if this is someone who will care for and respect you, the audience does the same to you. They're sizing you up, and your opening message tells everyone so much about what's to come and confirms if everyone should hang around for more or go in search of the exit.

Convey confidence at the start of your presentation by saying these two words: thank you. The power of this is, in this instance, you are not saying "thank you" out of obligation, but you are using it in its true form as an expression of respect. The underlying message is you expect to receive kindness from the audience during your presentation, and you are thanking everyone in advance for that kindness and respect. (In the spirit of keeping it real, the unspoken message is "I've got a big job to do up here. Don't mess with me!")

Do not waste time with your biography, an introduction of yourself, background stories, or talking about how nervous you are.[2] Give the audience what it came to get; your talk was publicized before your arrival, and there are key points you promised to deliver. Give them what was promised in that publicization.[3] If you've ever seen me present, then you know exactly how this is done. When you hear me say "By the time we're done, you will know...," I'm giving you a reason to listen. This is said within the first few minutes of the presentation and before I even tell you my name.[4]

REAL TALK PRINCIPLE

Immediately give everyone a reason to want to lean in and listen to you.

Second, practice your presentation full-out as if the audience is right there with you. I am so serious about this because it is precisely what I do. When I write "full-out," it is synonymous to a theatrical dress rehearsal. Full-out practice means you do not go through the motions or mentally think through what you will say. You give the presentation as if it is the actual performance, pausing for the audience interaction that will take place, making the asides, moving with purpose—all of that. Practice your presentation in an empty room, full-out, and a minimum of three times, and you will feel like a rockstar when it is time for you to deliver. Even if you have never before made the presentation, it will sound like it is your signature talk that you have been performing for years because you will have already performed it multiple times, in preparation for the audience to consume it.

Again, practice in an empty room, not in front of a mirror, so you HEAR what your audience will hear and feel what your audience will feel. (If you are dying to see what you look like, then engage a camera to record yourself. Ensure that you are not acting for the camera, though. Remain focused on the presentation performance itself. Pay attention to what you say and how you say it. Endeavor to give your listeners the kind of experience you would want to have if you were in the audience.) Do that a minimum of three times, and the nerves will be reduced.

Short on time?

Deliver the first 10 minutes and the last 10 minutes full-out a minimum of three times in your practice. Nail those first 10 minutes and the last 10 and you set-up yourself for success and you are able to close with power. You know what will come out of your mouth; hence, you are not afraid of what you will say—you have heard it before because in order to take control of how you look, how you sound, what you say, and how you say it, then those opening and closing minutes are when you must be at your best. Think to yourself, "If the audience remembers nothing else, I want them to remember the first thing and the last thing I say."

Check out *Show Up and Show Out: 52 Communication Habits to Make You Even More Unforgettable* for more on taking control of you look, how you sound, what you say, and how you say it.

---

[1]For more on adding jokes to your presentation, see "Why No One Laughs When You Crack a Joke and What to Do Instead" in chapter 3.

[2]For more on biographies and introductions, see "The Way You Have Been Introducing Yourself to Your Audiences is All Wrong" as well as "No Impressive Bio or Background? No Problem!" in chapter 2.

[3]How to give your audience what was promised is covered in chapter 3.

[4]For more on creating an unstoppable intro to your presentation, see "The One and Only Way to Ever Start Your Presentation" in chapter 3.

YOUR SPEECH MAY BE A VICTIM
OF WIMPY WORDS

You have heard and seen them before: those colleagues who sound infinitely confident and commanding. Their voices and their presence seemingly fill the room. They are always called upon to give speeches. They always seem to have the right thing to say.

Is this because they were Communication majors in college?

Or are they naturally great communicators?

Or incredibly confident?

Possibly.

But the truth is it could be none of those at play. And I know what's up. I have the secret sauce. And what you're not going to believe is you already have the secret sauce yourself! (See? Other experts won't tell you this!)

Their secret is word choice.

That's it.

Word choice.

Think about it.

Rev. Dr. Martin Luther King, Jr. did not say "I think I may have seen something in my sleep." Rather, he said "I have a dream!" In his January 20, 1961 Inaugural Address to the nation, President John F. Kennedy did not proclaim to each American to "Think about what you might be able to do for your country." He clarified that you should "ask not what your country can do for you—ask what you can do for your country"! Oprah didn't say "There's a possibility you might get a set of wheels today." Absolutely not! You know what she said! Say it with me: "You get a car! YOU GET A CAR!"

REAL TALK PRINCIPLE

When you choose strong words rather than wimpy words, you sound infinitely more confident and commanding.

When you choose weak words, you sound and look weak and uncertain, and weakness is that on which the jitters feed.[1]

Powerful speakers—even in impromptu, unscripted moments— use words that convey strength. That is, in large part, what builds confidence and eradicates the butterflies. That is what makes audiences sit up and listen. That is how powerful speakers make a statement and indisputably compel us to pay more and more attention. You want to tune in because these speakers instantly give you the right feeling; they sound like they believe and have conviction in what they are saying. This causes *you* to have the same belief and conviction. When you speak with belief and with conviction, then your listeners believe in you; they feel your conviction.

However, when your audience hears your uncertainty—your belief that you might…uh…be able to maybe pull that off one day, then you see the strange looks formulate in the crowd, which causes your anxiety to go way up. When the audience hears you delicately moving through details as opposed to assertively using strong words, then the audience is unsure. The audience is unsure of your strength, and the audience is unsure of your ability to get the job done. This energy transfers to you, and you start to feel unsure.

Get rid of wimpy words and weak phrases. Replace them with powerful speech. Speak with assertion, and choose words that follow suit.

CHART 1: Transform Wimpy Words Into Power Words

"I hope…"	BECOMES	"I trust…"
"I think…"	BECOMES	"I know…"
"I may/might…"	BECOMES	"I will…"
"I suggest…"	BECOMES	"I recommend…"
"I want to share…"	BECOMES	"I will discuss…" or "We will cover…"
"I believe that's it."	BECOMES	"That brings us to our conclusion."
"I don't know…"	BECOMES	"That is a question I must research."
"If…"	BECOMES	"When…" or "By [this date]…"

Continued

CHART 1: Transform Wimpy Words Into Power Words
(Continued)

"Worried…"	BECOMES	"Concerned…"
"Problem…"	BECOMES	"Challenge…"
"I'll try…"	BECOMES	"I will…" or "I am committed…"
"Sort of…" "Kind of…"	BECOMES	"It is…"
"Might…" or "Perhaps…"	BECOMES	"Definitely…" or "Absolutely…"

Still not convinced? Consider the following sentence pairs, read them aloud, and decide which gives the better, stronger, more confident impression. Seriously. Make sure you read them aloud. I won't interrupt you.

CHART 2: Which is Stronger?

1	I hope this was helpful.	I trust this was helpful.
2	I may be able to do that.	I can do that.
3	I suggest we share this with others.	I recommend we discuss this with others.

Avoid tiptoeing through the tulips, roaming through the roses, or dancing around the daisies. Say what you have to say with confidence and conviction.

---

[1]Using filler words such as "uh" and "um" also signal weakness and diminish confidence. Read more about filler words and how to reduce your use of them in "8 Secrets to Adjust Your Use of 'Uh,' 'Um,' and Other Filler Words" in chapter 1.

8 SECRETS TO ADJUST YOUR USE OF "UH," "UM," AND OTHER FILLER WORDS

Filler words, also called verbal segregates, are a part of everyday speech. We hear professionals use them—even news anchors and reporters whose primary industry tool is their ability to effectively communicate via the spoken word. We use them all the time. Filler words occur in our speech because we are trying to think of what we want to say next, and that thought process verbalizes itself in the form of a filler word. The mere use of filler words is not bad. It becomes problematic when you use them too often, serving to weaken your message and diminish your credibility. A repeated use of filler words makes you sound unsure, ultimately crushing your confidence.

However, depending upon your audience, incorporating them into your conversation is perfectly fine. Note I indicated "conversation," not "presentation." When conversing with those from a younger generation, an increased frequency with which you use filler words is acceptable. However, when making a formal presentation—regardless of the audience's age—remain cognizant of your use of filler words.

Examples of filler words are "uh," "um," "well," "like," "so," "actually," "you know," "really," "right," "all right," and "okay" (which is also lazily articulated as "'kay," "m'kay," or "n'kay"). These words vary person to person, so you have to pay attention to your own speech and know which ones you use before you work to reduce how much you use them.

Notice I wrote "reduce" and not "eliminate." I do not recommend you completely delete all filler words from your vocabulary, as you will learn in the first suggestion below. In all honesty—and yes, that phrase is one of my fillers!—the sparing use of filler words makes you sound human! However, if you allow them to creep into your speech too often, overclouding everything you say, then these words weaken your message and make you feel and sound anxious. Therefore, you have to decide how often you use filler words, whether the frequency needs to be reduced, and which ones you want to totally eliminate from your speech.

1. Decide which filler words you want to eliminate.

Do not endeavor to eliminate all filler words from your vocabulary. If you are unsure of which filler words you use, then to get an assessment, consciously listen to yourself every time you speak, record yourself making a presentation, and note how many times you hear filler words. Another option is to ask a friend or a trusted colleague to listen to you either in the course of casual conversations or during a formal presentation and tally the number of times you use filler words when you speak. Determine if there are one or two filler words you use in heavy rotation, then decide that you will focus on eliminating those words from your vocabulary—or at least focusing on significantly reducing your use of them. As you work to lessen their appearance in your speech, do not call attention to what you are doing by saying, "Oh! I'm trying to stop saying 'like' so much." Just do it.

2. Slow it down.

We think faster than we speak, and nervousness causes you to speed up your speech. As a result, we often say filler words when our minds are working to catch up with our mouths. The best fix for this is to slow down your speech. Not only does this help with lessening your use of filler words, but it also helps you sound more articulate.

Now, there are times when speed with speech is good, such as when you show excitement. However, if the entire presentation is going at warp speed, then the nerves are definitely doing the talking for you. The ideal rate of speech for public speaking is 140 to 180 words per minute. Any slower, and it's boring. Any faster, and you sound like you're trying to get this over—and fast! To check your rate, either record a few minutes of your talk with your smartphone (or any other recording device) or watch one of your own videos. If you use a mobile device, make sure you convert your speech to text. Talk for one minute to capture the text, then cut and paste the text into a word counter. There are several no-cost and at-cost tools out there to help you accomplish this. Conduct an Internet search for "convert speech to text" to see the options available to you.

You avoid filler words also by chunking; this is where you say a chunk of words, pause and breathe (which helps with voice projection), then say another chunk of information. What's happening here is you are forced to slow down your speech by strategically inserting pauses to develop a rhythm.[1]

3. Pause and say nothing.

The next time you feel a filler word getting ready to make an appearance, pause and say nothing. Seriously. No one will even notice. It will come off as a contemplative pause or a dramatic pause for effect, and it is my favorite go-to strategy. I'm serious. I use it. All. The. Time. This technique works best at the start or the end of a sentence rather than in the middle, but it is perfectly fine to use it mid-sentence. Bear in mind, if you pause for more than a half a second or so while in the middle of a sentence, it confuses people as they will wonder if your intent is to end the sentence in mid-thought. Start practicing this by simply pausing after every sentence you say; this gets you accustomed to the idea of this silence that may initially seem weird and awkward. You will soon realize that it's not even a big deal!

And this works with caveats, too. Caveats are those little explanations people will provide at the starts of sentences, and they make you sound weak. Do you ever begin your sentences with "This is just my opinion," or "Sorry," or "I'm still working on this," or "Well," or "I mean," or any number of other negative or useless prefaces? Most people do this as a matter of habit or nervousness, but caveats and filler words damage confidence. Instead, pause and say nothing in the place of the caveat—essentially, delete the caveat—then say what you mean and nothing else.

> More about the impact caveats have on your message is covered in *Show Up and Show Out: 52 Communication Habits to Make You Even More Unforgettable*. To sound assertive and sure of yourself when you speak, delete the caveat or preface, and begin your sentence where the preface would end.

4. Look your listener in the eyes.

When you look into a person's eyes, it is awkward to say "um." Therefore—and it is simply good practice—make great eye contact when you speak. As such, you are less likely to use filler words.

5. Prepare and practice for upcoming meetings, not just presentations.

Not only do people use filler words when they are trying to think of what they want to say next, but they subconsciously use filler words as if they are transition words. For instance, when getting ready to move on to the next agenda item, one might say "okay" as a filler as opposed to simply saying "Let's go to our next agenda item." (Note: This becomes bothersome when "okay" is the transition for everything on the agenda.) If you're leading a meeting, then plan the transitional phrases you will use. Consider "let's move on to …" or—and I love to use this one—"excellent" in order to reduce the likelihood that you will use filler words.

6. Use your entire body when you talk.

When you cannot (or do not) move your hands as you speak, you feel restrained and less confident about your message. Consequently, when you feel less confident about your message, you tend to use more filler words. So, get that head a-movin' and those hands to flailin'! I'm kidding, but seriously—use your body to your advantage when you speak. Gesticulate as you speak in order to punctuate your words, to tell your full story, and to put confidence in your words. When you do that, it is less likely you will utter filler words.

7. Project your voice.

When you project your voice, you project confidence. When you project confidence, you are less likely to use filler words.

To project your voice, fill your diaphragm before you speak. When you inhale and your midsection expands, you know you are filling your diaphragm. That is what you want. When you inhale and your shoulders rise, you're filling your lungs. You do not want that. It's that air in your diaphragm that positions you to project your voice.

Think about it: Would you take a deep breath, then loudly and energetically say "uh"? LOL! Not likely. It doesn't feel (or sound!) right. So, you won't do it if you are projecting your voice. Project your voice, and you project confidence. Project confidence, and you reduce your use of filler words.

8. Make it a habit.

Meetings and presentations are not the only places where you should work to eliminate your use of filler words. If you make it a habit to reduce your usage of them and make a point to focus on always being an effective communicator when you are in social settings, out and about, running errands, and the like, then it becomes far easier to not use filler words when you are in those professional settings. So, when you're at the grocery store; post office; or bank talking to the cashier, mail carrier, or teller, use the aforementioned techniques. And when you do that before taking to the stage, it is far easier to not use filler words!

---

[1]For more on how to insert pauses into your presentations, see "The Power of the Pause: 9 Types of Pauses You Need to Add to Your Presentations" in chapter 3.

MAKE THIS ONE CHANGE TO SOUND CONFIDENT EVERY SINGLE TIME YOU SPEAK

I hear it in certain circles more than others, and most people do not even realize or hear they are committing the offense. It shatters others' confidence in you or, at a minimum, makes it difficult for others to hear the substance of your message.

What is it?

Uptalk.

Uptalk is also called high-rising terminal, and it creeps into more people's speech than you can imagine even when they are not on a microphone, making formal presentations. Uptalk is when you articulate a statement seemingly as a question; there is a lilt to your voice as you get to the end of each sentence or to the end of a thought, and while it is not intentional, it has a negative impact on the power of your message. Arguably, the most significant problems with uptalk is ...

1. it causes your listeners to tune you out or miss vital parts of your message; and

2. it signals to hecklers in the audience that you can be railroaded.

But why does uptalk happen in the first place?

1. One reason it happens is because you are in search of approval by the audience—in search of acceptance of your ideas. And the search reveals itself in a change in the tone of your voice.

2. It also occurs because you subconsciously use it to indirectly check the listener's understanding of what you said. In this instance, the uptalk is synonymous with you saying, at the end of your sentence, "Does that make sense?"

3. A third reason it occurs is because some people subconsciously think it makes them sound more interesting as they speak, that it adds variety to their voices. And it does add variety, just not in a good way.

4. Next, uptalk happens because you are excited and are rushing to get to the next thought.

5. Finally, uptalk surfaces when you are afraid of the words coming out of your mouth, especially if you are about to deliver bad news. The last words of your sentence are spoken with a pensiveness, and it sounds like you are afraid to fully voice to your ideas.

If you are unsure of whether you use uptalk, listen very closely to yourself when you speak. Search for that lilt in your voice at the ends of sentences, listen to a recording of yourself, or ask a trusted colleague to listen and give you feedback.

Once you identify that you are using uptalk, you fix it by finishing your statements mentally and verbally before moving on to the next point. End with a period, not a question mark. The second fix is to ensure you use your ideal speaking voice every time you speak. To find your ideal speaking voice, hum the "Happy Birthday" song. Just the first three syllables of the first line of the song will do—"Happy bir." The tone at which you hum those first three syllables is the tone of your ideal speaking voice. Go on. Hum. Do it now. I'll wait.

REAL TALK PRINCIPLE

When you use your ideal speaking voice and eliminate uptalk, you have a commanding sound to your speech.

When your voice is commanding, hecklers remain quiet, and everyone pays attention. To show strength and conviction and to sound confident when you speak, eliminate uptalk so the sound of your voice takes you from being viewed as just another run-of-the-mill presenter to being viewed as a respected professional.

HOW TO USE NONVERBAL COMMUNICATION TO SILENTLY COMMUNICATE YOUR CONFIDENCE

Your presentation starts before you say a word, and your body makes a statement that goes beyond what your actual words say. When you strategically use your nonverbal communication, your presentation anxiety is significantly reduced. Trust me on this one.

REAL TALK PRINCIPLE

Your presentation starts before you say a word.

Here are questions to ask yourself to determine how well your body language is positively impacting your audience members' interest and engagement and how well it is enhancing your overall presence as a powerhouse at the front of the room:

Do you...

1. stand at the front and center of the room and stand still in one position to address everyone at the start of your presentation?

2. not begin speaking until all talking in the audience has ceased and you have everyone's attention?

3. hold your head high with your shoulders back?

4. use appropriate facial expressions?

5. use a variety of hand gestures to emphasize the points you make?

6. move about the room throughout the presentation?

If you do, then your body language says...

1. you want to stand in a position where you are able to see everyone and command everyone's attention (and keep in mind you should never address the back of your audience; if you are at the back of the room and need to address the audience, make your way to the front and address everyone from there);

2. you insist on the respect you and your message are due, and you will not compete for attention;

3. you look confident and ready to engage in the business of learning and thinking;

4. you have personality and will bring it to the presentation;

5. you are energetic and passionate about your message; and

6. you are intent on monitoring the room and keeping high the level of attention among your audience members as well as the attention you given them in return.

To help keep your body language under control, imagine a box in front of your chest and belly.

1. To signal CONFIDENCE, contain all your hand movements within the aforementioned box.

2. To signal that you FEEL IN CONTROL, stand with your feet about a shoulder width apart.

3. To signal CONFIDENCE AND CONTROL, gesture as if you are holding a basketball between your hands.

4. To signal STRENGTH, AUTHORITY, and ASSERTIVENESS, gesture with the palms of your hands facing downward.

5. To signal YOU ARE RELAXED, clasp both hands together in a relaxed pyramid.

6. To signal OPENNESS AND HONESTY, gesture with the palms of your hands up.

These points are also covered in chapter 4, but it simply makes sense to have them here, too, since you are encouraged to use appropriate body language as a part of building your confidence.

Before going on, practice all six of these right now. Go on. I'll wait.

Next, smile when you present. It is contagious. Not only does this make you sound more pleasant, but it gives you an air of confidence. A smile is synonymous with being friendly, approachable, and composed. Besides, it looks far better than a frown, does it not?!

Finally, be comfortable with silence. For one, it is a powerful confidence-booster. Additionally, silence gives audience members time to let your ideas sink in. Remember, they are hearing your ideas for the first time; they need that time to hear and understand your ideas. As such, stop worrying when you initially get silence from the audience when you ask a question. You have to allow for silence so audience members have time to think, process the question, and arrive at an answer. Remember when you demonstrate you are comfortable with momentary instances of silence, it also shows you are confident.

WHY YOU FREEZE ON STAGE AND HOW TO FIX IT

There are two reasons fear appears and you freeze on stage. One, it's because you do not speak on a stage every day. Plain and simple. Think about it: The less you engage in a practice, the harder it is to do it. (Exercising … eating healthy foods … thinking positive thoughts … all of those are tough if you do not perform them on a regular basis.) Second, you freeze when you do not have choreography in place; you freeze when you do not have a game plan.

News anchors. Emcees. TV show hosts. Professional comedians. Commencement speakers. Professional speakers. Company spokespersons. All of them sound so clear and confident when you hear them speak. Are they naturally gifted communicators? Yes, some of them are. Are they professionally trained? That's possible, too. Are they able to just speak off the cuff? Sure, there are persons with that talent.

However, that is not the case with everyone. This is what the best speakers do: They write scripts and use them as the basis for what they say. That way, they are not freezing on stage, and they are not searching for their words, they are not stumbling over their words, scrambling to remember the points they want to make. Well before it is time to present, they write a script. Then they go over it and over it and over it so they know it so well that when they get on a stage, they do not freeze. They know it so well that when they see several sets of eyes staring back at them, they know precisely what they plan to say.

Writing a script may initially seem like a tedious amount of work, but it will keep you from freezing. You will know your presentation like the back of your hand. This is how you get through it: Ask yourself "If I was writing a letter to a friend about this information, then what would I write?" Then start writing that letter! And write with a strong belief; you must have a deep belief in what you write (and then say) to eliminate the possibility of freezing up. What you write, with plans to present it to your audience, has to be material that resonates with you. This way, if you have a momentary lapse in memory or are distracted by a look from an audience member, you are able to easily get back on track as a result of being both intellectually and emotionally tied to the topic. Look at this as an opportunity to communicate, not an opportunity to perform. Although, let's be clear; you are performing. First and foremost, though, you are communicating with the goal of transforming people, not putting on a show for others to critique you.

So, back to writing the script. At the start, do not worry about organization, transitions, punctuation, grammar, or mechanics because 1) you can go back and fix all of that later and 2) even if you do not return to correct the errors, none of it matters anyway because this is for your eyes only. All that matters is that you are able to understand your thoughts What is most critical, in this moment, is that you put pen to paper (or fingertips to the keyboard) and get your thoughts out so you know everything it is you want to say. They can be in paragraph form or a list of bullets—do what works for you.

After you get everything down, organize your thoughts, edit, and revise as need be. Then you are ready to rehearse and practice. With a script in place, you are able to stand on that stage, command your audience, and effortlessly communicate your ideas without freezing, feeling the jitters, or losing your train of thought.[1] (Now bear in mind, you will not take the script on stage with you and read it to your audience. You have your script there with you as a reference point in the event you have a momentary loss of thought; however, you will not stand and read it to your audience—unless that is the event expectation.[2] [If it is, then you don't have to worry about seeing me in the audience!] You will have practiced your script so much until you know it by heart. And it is perfectly acceptable if you veer off script or if you ad lib here and there. You will have your major points down because you wrote them then rehearsed them.)

Going forward, before your next presentation, and before you even begin to add graphics or to design your presentation, write your script. Just know the first few times will be challenging, but it gets easier and easier the more you do it.

---

[1] But to prepare yourself in case you you *do* lose your train of thought, see "What to Do if You Lose Your Train of Thought" in chapter 1.

[2] If you are an exceptionally skilled reader who can read in a way that is not robotic, then you may very well be able to get away with this on a webinar.

WHAT TO DO IF YOU LOSE YOUR TRAIN OF THOUGHT

One time, while on a flight from Dallas to Shreveport, I have no idea what possessed me to drop my phone into the literature compartment located on the back of the seat in front of me. I'm sure it was one of those moments we've all experienced where we need a third hand, and in that moment, that little pocket became my third hand. But...here's the problem...the phone disappeared! Before letting go of it, it didn't occur to me *where* it would go!

It had seemingly vanished into a space that, in my mind, would require the seat to be completely disassembled to retrieve it, and I had a flash of panic! You know how your face gets hot and you feel a quiver in your chest? That's how I was feeling.

I gasped and, with lightning speed, snapped to turn my head to the left and give a "Did you see that?!" look to my seat mate who—immediately sympathizing with me—also had a look of desperation wash over his previously calm and friendly face. Our shock was short-lived for as quickly as I'd dropped the phone into the literature holder did I have the presence of mind to turn the latch that held my tray table in place, let down the tray, and there was my phone nestled behind an unused trash/barf bag, partially visible through one of the openings on the seat. However, if that had not happened, I'd already made up my mind that I was going to ask for professional help and keep myself parked on that plane until that phone was rescued! (But had my husband, Aaron, been with me, he would have casually and coolly opened the tray table without giving any of this a second thought. He's such a smooth operator ... *cue Sade*)

So ... when you lose your thought in your presentation, do the same thing I did:

Find a friendly face.

Search for an opening.

Ask for help.

1. Find a friendly face.

It helps to make a friend or two before the start of your presentation. Roam the room and chat with participants before the official start time, stand at the entrance to shake hands with participants as they enter the room, or—and this is a personal favorite of mine—answer audience questions until it's time to start. When you engage in any one of these, you will find a someone who instantly becomes your cheerleader. When you lose your thought, find that friendly face with the goal and hope of it calming you and helping you get back on track.

2. Search for an opening.

Cruising the audience, chatting it up, or taking questions before you speak may not be your style. I get it. Keep your notes handy so you can have an opening. With them nearby, you can easily reference them if you lose where you were going with your presentation. Additionally, if you use slides, use the presenter view so you can see your notes without them being projected to the audience. Or include great images in your slide deck; glancing at one of those great images you have displayed can be that opening you need to jog your memory and get you back on course.

3. Ask for help.

Audiences do not want to see you fail. They really don't. If you find yourself in a pickle, in search of the next words you were going to say, say "Somebody, help me out. What was the last thing I said before I went on that tangent?" or "Where did I leave off before we started that great discussion?" There will be someone in the audience who's willing to oblige and who will tell you exactly what you said last.

THE BIG MISTAKE EVERYONE MAKES WHEN IT COMES TO INTROVERTS AND PUBLIC SPEAKING

We are inclined to believe extroverts are the more skilled and the more confident presenters when compared to their introverted counterparts, but … hold the phone.

While words appear to come more easily for our extroverted friends who gain their energy from being around others, introverts are missing out if they (and others) believe they are not serious contenders as speakers.

The one mistake introverts make and the dangerous misconception held by so many is assuming introverts are not gifted and confident speakers. Quite to the contrary, we (Yes, "we"—yours truly is an introvert through and through.) may be even more talented on the mic than others. Here are three reasons why.

1. Introverts are incredibly self-aware, and this bodes well for their speaking.

Before they utter a thought, introverts carefully scrutinize their words and ideas, paying keen attention to the entire packaging of their messaging. They are not quick to take to a microphone without first carefully analyzing any combination of their appearance, body language and other nonverbal communication, and/or how they want their message to be received. As such, during impromptu moments when called upon to "say a few words," they are not eager to speak up *not* because they do not have anything to say; it's because they have not had ample opportunity to organize their thoughts and ensure they produce a quality message—even if it *is* to say only a few words.

They want to think before they speak; they want what they say to be carefully scripted in their minds so when it is verbalized, there is little to no room for them to look or sound less than polished. Now, let me be abundantly clear. This is not to suggest extroverts are not sensitive to the quality of their messages; they simply require far less time to organize their thoughts and, quite honestly, they prefer speaking during *un*scripted moments. They are the ones who do not need a PowerPoint deck and can crush it! But because of introverts' inclination to examine and re-examine most of what they plan to say before they verbalize it, their self-awareness and acute attention to detail can result in them being quite talented during formal speaking engagements.

2. Introverts like to build their skills in private as opposed to jumping in feet first.

This is particularly advantageous for introverts because they are comfortable being in a room alone and are, therefore, more likely to practice for their presentations in the one and only way one should ever practice, which is to deliver presentations all alone while out of sight of others and full-out as if there *is* an audience watching.

A mistake many speakers make is mentally going through their presentations and dubbing it as having practiced, but introverts are less likely to make this mistake. By conducting a dress rehearsal in private and without distractions, they hear the words they plan to articulate in front of the live audience. Once you hear the words, see the gestures, and get a sense of the flow of the presentation, you know where to fix lulls, how to ensure the audience is engaged, and whether your message is on-track. Knowing all of this and, more importantly, addressing it during practice and well before showtime results in a presentation that is methodically and thoughtfully delivered with intention.[1]

3. Introverts' preference for learning by listening intently, paying attention to others, and making discoveries through observation gives them a true advantage on the stage.

If there is any guarantee with any presentation, it is that your audience *will* give you a reaction without saying a word. Introverts' astute attention to others' nonverbal communication and introverts' tendency to be great observers is a plus in the presentation environment because if they sense a positive vibe from the audience, then they know they are on the right trajectory; however, if the body language tells them otherwise, then they know they need to do or say something different and do or say it quickly to avoid losing the momentum they have built.

Rather than committing to delivering the message at all costs while ignoring any telltale signs of negativity from audience members, if and when placed in a scenario where multiple audience members appear less than satisfied with the message, introverts are better positioned to learn from these reactions.

They will assess their content and its delivery, then endeavor to offer points of clarification or opportunities for the audience to provide feedback, thereby, keeping the message on target.

Simply put, if one is an introvert, it does not mean one is *not* destined to make stellar presentations, and it does not mean you should not have utmost confidence in your abilities. Actually, an introvert may be quite the thoughtful and organized speaker with a heightened sense of awareness of audience needs. Popular beliefs or widely accepted attitudes will suggest extroverts are positioned to give the best speaking performances; however, it's time for a paradigm shift because—let's be clear— introverts are wired to rock the mic just as well as—if not better than!—anyone else.

---

[1]For more on how to engage in more effective means of practicing, see "Why You Get Nervous Before a Presentation and the Expert Practice Strategy Guaranteed to Change That" in chapter 1.

HOW TO FEARLESSLY PRESENT
IN FRONT OF COWORKERS

Why does it seem easier to present in front of strangers than in front of your coworkers? (Or am I all alone on this one?)

One would think the latter is an ideal situation. These are people who know you—people who will cheer you on; they are people before whom you do not need to prove yourself. Or ... are they?

Here is how to take the worry out of presenting in front of coworkers.

1. Pretend you are indeed in front of a room full of strangers.

This keeps you from getting too lax and then, not doing your absolute best. If you tell yourself "This is just another audience who is going to see me at my best" as opposed to "These are my coworkers," you better position yourself to remain aware of every move you make and every word you say. You see, when you keep saying to yourself "these are just my teammates," you might get too comfortable and feel as though you do not have to put on your best performance. This is quite to the contrary. If anything, this is the time when you want to put on the very best performance possible, illustrating the very best version of yourself! And this leads to my next point.

2. Call upon your inner thespian.

Pretend your teammates are complete strangers, and show your teammates how it is done and how it is done right. From start to finish, demonstrate your presentation skills knowledge and abilities as well as your industry-specific chops. Own your expertise. Show them how polished you are!

3. Do not feel like you must be funny.

Often presenters become concerned if no one is laughing or smiling during their presentations; they think it is not going well. Wrong. That is not necessarily the case. First, you are not a comedian. Remember the goal of your presentation is to coherently and professionally show your insights in an organized fashion. Period.[1]

4. Save questions for the end.

It is enough of a challenge to keep track of everything you want to say and how you want to say it, even with notes and preparation, but having teammates interrupt you with questions during your presentation brings the potential of making everything more difficult. Simply let everyone know at the start of your presentation that you will take questions at the end, and encourage each person to jot down questions as they come to them. You may actually end up answering many of those questions for them as you present. In other instances, I will indicate you have the option to take questions throughout, at designated points, or at the end of a presentation.[2] When presenting to team members who are likely already comfortable with you, the chance they will get you off your game is heightened. Therefore, control for this as much as possible by getting through your entire presentation before letting anyone sidetrack or distract you with questions.

5. Do not feel the need to say everything.

You will not be able to anyway. You might worry that your teammates will call you on to the carpet because you did not include every single detail. Take heart that if you did, your presentation would likely be too long, and you would lose people. Commit to addressing three to five topics, depending on the time you have. You always have the option to answer questions offline. You work in the same place, right? Therefore, you can easily arrange for follow-up conversations.

And by the way, if this is a presentation that is not directed at your teammates but is one where your teammates will be in the audience either awaiting their turn to present or simply as a matter of formality, pretend they are not there or that their attendance is of no consequence. Focus all your energy on the rest of the audience, and again, show your teammates how to make an astoundingly beautiful presentation. Have them thinking, "I want to be exactly like her when I get on the mic!"

---

[1]For more on adding jokes to your presentation, see "Why No One Laughs When You Crack a Joke and What to Do Instead" in chapter 3.

[2]For more on when to take questions during your presentation, see "Stop Taking Questions at the End of Your Presentation" in chapter 5.

REFLECT, REVIEW, AND RESPOND: DO YOU KNOW HOW TO BUILD YOUR CONFIDENCE AND CRUSH THE JITTERS?

1. What causes a speaker to become nervous before a presentation? What should one do to control the jitters?

2. What wimpy words do you need to remove from your speech?

3. How effective is your presentation practice? What changes do you need to make with the way you practice?

4. Which filler words do you need to reduce your use of or completely eliminate from your speech, and how will you make that happen?

5. What is uptalk, and why is it problematic? Do you engage in uptalk? How do you confirm whether you engage in uptalk, and how do you reduce it?

6. What are examples of effective body language during presentations? What changes, if any, do you need to make to your body language?

7. What are the reasons speakers freeze on stage, and what should one do to make positive adjustments?

8. What are three strategies for regaining your train of thought when you present?

9. What is your plan, going forward, for presenting in front of your coworkers?

Chapter 2

ESTABLISH YOUR CREDIBILITY

Chapter 2

ESTABLISH YOUR CREDIBILITY

Your biography, résumé, long list of accomplishments, or your job title is not what establishes your credibility, and on their own, none of them will impress your audience.

Sure, they may demonstrate that you have experience, that you have perseverance, and that you have made progresses in your life. However, they do not immediately demonstrate credibility to your audience nor that you can take all that expertise and deliver it in a way that will bring about an engaging experience for your listeners. You establish your credibility with your audience by immediately communicating in your opening words that you are not there to just talk but that you are there to expertly deliver a carefully choreographed message, which thereby gives your audiences reason after reason to lean in and listen to you.

You are about to know how to ...

- create and execute a solid, strong, succinct introduction of yourself that establishes your credibility regardless of whether you have an impressive résumé or not
- clarify for your listeners what you do and why they should care
- give everyone a reason to prepare to listen to and respect every single word you say

THE WAY YOU HAVE BEEN INTRODUCING YOURSELF TO YOUR AUDIENCE IS ALL WRONG

Do you know the number one reason adults will listen to you? Why will an audience lean in with rapt attention? What will prompt them to get off their devices and turn their minds and eyes toward you?

Here it is: The number one reason adults will listen to you is because they know *why* they should listen to you.

Before you say your name and before you tell the audience what you do, tell everyone what he or she will know or be able to do by the end of your presentation. Then tell everyone how he or she will get there. In fact, if you have ever seen me present, this is precisely how I start all my sessions. I tell you exactly how your time will be spent. Doing so establishes credibility.

Time is a person's most precious commodity. Busy professionals need and want to know right away—not what your title is—but that what you are about to do is not speak for the sake of speaking but that you are speaking for the sake of helping them with what they do. Do not assume you have everyone's attention by the mere fact everyone is gathered to hear you. Assume you must blow them away and make them feel like "Wow. She means business. She's for real. Let me see what she's talking about."

There are two parts to moving your audience towards this kind of reaction. One is clarifying for the audience what it will know or be able to do once you finish your presentation.[1] The second part is revising how you let the audience know who you are—and that is what you are about to do now.

Even if someone delivers your introduction before handing the mic to you—literally or figuratively—still introduce yourself in your own words. Doing so accomplishes a number of things.

1. It gives you yet another chance to plug your name into the minds of the audience.

2. The audience hears you say the most important words associated with you, and that is your name!

3. You have the chance to establish the kind of power and energy that *you* want to be heard and felt behind your name.

You have heard introductions of you that were pretty good and others that were ... well ... meh. By taking control and providing for yourself a solid introduction, no matter how another person may have introduced you, you take control of your brand and how you want the audience to see, hear, and know you. To do this, you have to identify what it is the audience does and what it wants. You must also identify what you do, then bridge the gap.

Once you have those two pieces of information it is time to create a new power introduction that you will use every time you make a presentation in order to establish your credibility, and that starts with throwing out your job title.

Usually, people introduce themselves on the stage with "My name is _____, and I am a [JOB TITLE]." Instead, you will now say, "My name is _____, and what I do is, I help (target audience) _____, _____, and _____."

As you identify the three ways you help your audience, choose the three that are going to sound the most delicious and the most attractive to your audience. Choose the three that demonstrate very clearly the impact you have in the world. Avoid getting incredibly technical and academic here. Do not pull items from your job description; they do not have meaning for your audience. Identify three characteristics that will make everyone say "What?! She can help me do THAT?! I'm all ears!!!"

Or perhaps you help your audience with only one aspect of their lives. However, you can help them develop that aspect in three incredible ways. That works, too.

For instance, when I make a presentation, you will hear me say "My name is Bridgett McGowen, and what I do is I help professionals be the most engaging, dynamic, incredible communicators ever." Did you pick up on that? I help with one aspect, but I help you develop your communication in three incredible ways.

Did you notice something else?

I did not give you a job title.

REAL TALK PRINCIPLE

Titles mean nothing, and they do not establish
your credibility.

You might say "Bridgett, if someone is—let's say—the president of an organization, that is impressive! That establishes
credibility!" Yes, it is impressive, but it does not establish one's
credibility—not until you prove to your listeners that you are
worth your title. You do that by demonstrating your ability to help
others in whatever capacity in which you work. It is not until then
that your credibility is on the road to becoming fully established.
We have vague ideas of what titles mean, but why make it difficult for the audience by saying "My name is Bridgett McGowen,
and I am the Director of Professional Development and Strategic
Alliances"? Your first question is "Okay. That's nice, but what is
it exactly you do?!" (By the way, I can crack on that title because
it's one I once had.) Instead, tell the audience what it is you do
that helps everyone assembled be better at what he or she does.

Keep in mind you want your introduction to be punchy. It needs
to be quick and easy to remember, hear, and understand, and it
should take no more than five to 10 seconds for you to say it. If
it's any longer, then the audience will get lost, tune out, or hear
only a portion of what you say. None of that is a winner.

Punctuate every important phrase to give your audience the
space to soak up what you say. Punctuating each phrase asserts

power. It says, "I firmly believe in what I'm saying, and I need you to firmly believe it, too."

Remember, even if you have already been introduced, still say this power introduction.

Thank the person for the introduction, greet the audience and thank the audience for its time. Then, give your power introduction.

Your introduction should look like this:

Thank you, Tom.

Hello, everyone, and thank you for your time.

My name is _____, and what I do is, I help (target audience) _____, _____, and _____.

With a power introduction like this, credibility will follow.[2]

Get rid of words that do you and/or your presentation no justice—delete diminishing diction and replace it with leader language. Diminishing diction is any messaging that takes away value from you, your objectives, and your audience. As you can imagine, leader language is the opposite; it's those words that light up a room and that cause your listeners to lean in and that make you look like—you guessed it—a leader.

And to take this a step further, avoid saying what you are not. Case in point, while I was attending a live YouTube session on book marketing tactics, the presenter included in his introduction that he is a book marketer but that he has never written a book.

Did the latter part of that statement cause a dip in some participants' confidence in him?

Possibly.

Is it a huge deal?

Not really.

But at the same time, I'm not so sure that his not being an author was relevant. If you know how to market books, dude, then you know how to market books! Own it! It's akin to the image of a slender yet successful chef. If you're good at what you do, then that's all that matters—there's no need to minimize yourself, but if someone asks about a credential or achievement, then be honest. But do not set the stage with what you are not or what you have not accomplished.

Owning your expertise and specific talents without minimizing what you do and who you are is covered more in *Show Up and Show Out: 52 Communication Habits to Make You Even More Unforgettable.*

---

[1]More on clarifying for the audience what it will know or be able to do is covered in chapter 3.

[2]There is more to the power intro. This is just to get you started. The full power intro is covered in "The One and Only Way to Ever Start Your Presentation" in chapter 3 and "The Only Presentation Plan You Will Ever Need Part 2: The Actual Presentation" in chapter 4.

THE BODY LANGUAGE THAT'S REQUIRED TO OWN THE ROOM

Do you find yourself pacing and moving around on stage just because you automatically do it? If so, then I need you to start being far more intentional with your movements. Do not just stroll around with no direction. This is especially key in the first few minutes of your presentation. In your opening words, keep all movement to an absolute minimum, and when you do move, move with purpose.

REAL TALK PRINCIPLE

When you move, move with purpose. Move as if you own the room or—better yet—as if you own the entire building.

If you simultaneously move and speak without syncing your words with your movement, then it gets in the way of the audience being able to pay 100 percent attention to your words.[1]

You will see speakers who are introduced before they present and, from a seated position, they will start speaking before they completely get out of their chairs. The legs of the chairs are still scraping across the floor, making distracting noises. And because of the position of their bodies, they are bent, looking slightly downward. Therefore, the floor hears them really really well—far better than anyone in the room hears them, especially if they are competing with the sound of chair legs scraping across hard-surfaced floors.

Wait until you are standing straight, have stopped walking, are in position, standing still, fully poised, and focused on your audience before you say a word.

Additionally, watch your grooming gestures—touching your hair, fumbling with an earring, adjusting your tie or cuffs, rubbing your nose, and the like. When overdone, this type of movement takes away from your credibility. Naturally, if a hair is in your face, obstructing your view, move it, but endeavor to have as many purposeful movements as possible.

Assume the power position, which is at the front and center of the room. At times, because of the setup of the room, it can be incredibly difficult or nearly impossible to assume this position to a "t." Do your best to get right in the center and at the front of the room.

If there is a lectern in a smaller setting, then it may not be positioned front and center. In those instances, start front and center, and if you must use the lectern, move in that direction after making your introduction. At the same time, be careful not to stand in the light of the projector if such equipment is in use. Standing in a position that obstructs any portion of the path of the light that's making its way from the projector's bulb to the screen is an amateur move. Again, it can be a challenge, but get as close to the front and center as possible.

In larger venues, the lectern is usually already positioned in this fashion; however, if it is not, then ensure you start in a position of prominence. If the lectern is over to the side but is on a stage or a podium, then that stage or podium is a position of prominence. Start there.[2]

Always speak clearly, enunciate each syllable, and look the entire audience in the eye. You make full eye contact with the audience by imagining a diamond shape over your audience; use this diamond to block your presentation's introduction.

a. When you start speaking, ensure you look in the center of the room.

b. From there, continue to look to left of the room for a few seconds.

c. Then to the right.

d. Then, look down front and center before...

e. You look to the back and center.

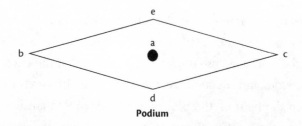

Podium

Repeat that pattern throughout your talk with your hands at your side; in a steepled position with your fingertips touching each other or clasped in front of your body; or if you are holding a microphone, hold it with one hand and have your other hand by your side. (But a pro move is to insist on a lavalier to free up your hands.)

Here's how that looks with your scripted power introduction:[3]

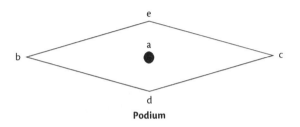

Podium

a. Look in the center (a) and say, "My name is _____."

b. Then look to the diamond's far left point (b) and say, "What I do is...."

c. Look to the diamond's far right point (c) and say, "I help _____."

d. Take your eyes to the front of the audience (d), the diamond's lower point, to state your second point.

e. And go to the back of the audience, the diamond's top point (e), for your final point. (Along with this final point, I typically add "Stop me at any time with your questions."[4])

Repeat this pattern with each point you make, either with your eyes or by moving your body to those positions. It gives purpose to your movements, and it ensures you give "everyone" eye contact. Offer no distractive moves that will take away from the audience hearing what you have to say.

---

[1]For more on body language, see "How to Use Nonverbal Communication to Silently Communicate Your Confidence" in chapter 1.

[2]Are you wondering if you should move from the lectern or off the stage or podium? See "Should You Stand on the Podium or Behind the Lectern?" in chapter 4.

[3]For information on your power introduction, see "The Way You Have Been Introducing Yourself is All Wrong" in chapter 2 and "The Only Presentation Plan You Will Ever Need Part 2: The Actual Presentation" in chapter 4.

[4]For more on when to take questions, see "Stop Taking Questions at the End of Your Presentation" in chapter 4.

DOES YOUR LOOK MATCH YOUR MESSAGE?

While in attendance at a local groundbreaking ceremony where there were only men on the stage—that's another story for a DE&I conversation—who were from the governor's office or who were high-ranking executives with the company that was breaking ground in the area, I noticed all the men were wearing dark-color suits—all of them except for one. That one jokingly said he had received an email message that indicated—given the hot temperatures expected that day—to leave his dark-colored suit in the closet. He went on to add that it appeared as though he was the only one who read and followed the directions of the memo. The commentary got a good chuckle from the crowd, but he knew how prominently his tan suit jacket stood out in the sea of navy-blue attire.

But think about it. How often do you see a professional businessman—a man of power, a man of authority—wear a light-color suit? Not too often, if ever. And if he does, we certainly hear about it!

Do you remember the August 28, 2014 Obama tan suit controversy?

Some thought it was rather trivial for the news to report on it while others chalked it up to a slow news day in search of some excitement, but it led to some digging that revealed two instances of Ronald Reagan sporting light-color suits during his time in the White House in 1982 and 1988—a look deemed too casual for the office for both men.

Secondly, how often do you see a man's bare arms or shoulders in professional settings? That is another rarity or completely non-existent occurrence. And if it did occur, what would be the general public's reaction? How much confidence would an audience engender in them? It would surely be questionable.

I recognize fashion is subjective, and styles are ever-changing. This is territory that constantly shifts, especially as we see more and more success stories who boldly show up wearing anything but three-piece suits to board meetings. Being who I am, I tend to have a different point of view and work hard to ensure I'm consistently taken seriously before I open my mouth. As such, these are my recommendations based on my personal experiences with the goal of gaining respect.

REAL TALK PRINCIPLE

Before you even open your mouth, your appearance is doing the talking for you.

During daytime hours, women are strongly encouraged to always cover their shoulders and wear dark colors, especially if presenting to a mixed gender audience. Remember more skin = less credibility. Dark colors are not a must, but keep them in mind if the rest of the room will be wearing conservative colors.

I recognize I will get pushback on this one. Many will accurately argue there are plenty of powerful women who wear sleeveless ensembles. And to them, I say, using my best Tupac impersonation, "I ain't mad at cha." My stance remains as follows: You may be the smartest, brightest, most accomplished person in the room, but upon first glance, people make split-second assumptions and judgments about you. According to Sylvie di Guisto, co-author of *The Image of Leadership: How Leaders Package Themselves to Stand Out for the Right Reasons*, people form an impression of you within the first seven seconds of seeing you. Fairly or unfairly. Accurately or inaccurately. As such, you want to control, as much as possible, the impression you make and the role that not only your words play in establishing your credibility but also the role your appearance plays.

For anyone making presentations in a formal or black-tie setting, at an after-five affair, or during a company picnic, for example, then naturally, you follow suit—no pun intended—with the attire that is acceptable, appropriate, and expected for the occasion. In these instances, keep modesty in mind. Now don't get me wrong. I am not a prude and have been known to enjoy a fiery outfit or two myself! However, the establishment of credibility happens before one even opens his or her mouth. When you walk onto the stage, take to the mic, and prepare to speak, the audience is sizing you up. Do not give anyone a reason to doubt your credibility.

> For more on appearance and attire, you'll like the "How You Look" section of *Show Up and Show Out: 52 Communication Habits to Make You Even More Unforgettable*.

HOW WELL DO YOU REALLY KNOW YOUR AUDIENCE?

You have heard it before: Prior to making a presentation, learn as much about the audience as possible. What you have not heard is the kind of information you need to gather that goes beyond the typical demographical details.

Gaining more in-depth information about your listeners positions you to know what to say and that which you need to delete from your script so you sound credible when you speak. With the right kind of audience analysis as part of your presentation preparation, you will know which points you should strongly emphasize, and you will know what might be hot topics that should be avoided. (Of course, politics, religion, and money are always off the table … unless, of course you are facilitating a financial planning workshop or faith-based retreat, but I digress. Besides, you know what I mean!)

When you learn as many details as possible about the audience beforehand, you have a good idea of how much foundational information you should provide. You also know how deep of a dive you need to take with establishing definitions and a framework so everyone is on the same page. Okay. Sounds good, right? But how exactly is that done?

There are three stages involved when it comes to finding out who will be in your audience and how to work toward tailoring a message that will sow seeds of good ideas, resonate with your participants, and establish you as a credible speaker.

First Stage

Ask your event point of contact (POC) as many questions as possible about the audience—levels and numbers of years of experience in their industries, education levels, types of degrees attained (if applicable), age range, and job titles present in the audience. Those are the basics. Now set-up yourself for a successful display of credibility by getting more specifics: Find out the range of attitudes toward the presentation topic, specific challenges the audience has, and social and/or cultural considerations you may need to take under advisement. What are hot topics you should avoid? At the same time, what information have they been desperately craving? Even go so far as to ask the POC about sending a survey to prospective audience members beforehand, yielding results that will prove quite fruitful.

Second Stage

During the presentation, listen closely to responses participants give to your questions and/or the comments they make in response to the content you deliver. Your most valuable tool is to watch body language *very* closely. You can almost instantly tell how receptive a person is to a message by how he or she shifts in the chair, tilts his or her head, raises an eyebrow, looks down, frowns, or smiles. All these indicators are incredibly revealing. Based on what you learn during the presentation, make on-the-spot adjustments—not to appease but rather to improve the likelihood your message reaches the audience. These adjustments will also improve the likelihood you are able to compel the audience to take appropriate action.

Third Stage

Upon concluding your presentation, review all responses and reactions. Examine how well they align with the audience analysis you made based on the information you gained prior to the presentation. Then decide what adjustments, if any, you should make with future analyses before, during, and after your presentation.

> "Know Who's in Front of You" in *Show Up and Show Out: 52 Communication Habits to Make You Even More Unforgettable* gives you additional factors to consider when assessing your listeners and their needs.

NO IMPRESSIVE BIO OR BACKGROUND? NO PROBLEM!

How many times have you attended a presentation where the speaker was introduced via the reading of his or her biography? Or how many times have you been asked to provide your bio as a means of an introduction before you speak? How many times have you been in an audience where a speaker's bio was read, but you were not even listening.? People have long believed reading these bios, introductions, and the like will establish the speaker's credibility. Wrong. Wrong. Wrong. All wrong. And here's why:

As a standalone, your biography is not an effective means of establishing your credibility. It indicates what you have done but not what you can do right here, right now for the audience assembled before you. Granted, people may be impressed by your bio, and if that is the goal—to impress the audience—then bravo! But if the point is to establish credibility, then that bio does not do it.

REAL TALK PRINCIPLE

Your bio does not establish your credibility.

First, this is a speaker-centered approach, not an audience-centered approach. Second, the audience can—and often does—research the speaker online beforehand. Third, no one really listens to the reading of those bios. Fourth, even if there are attentive audience members who *do* listen, most of, if not all, the information is forgotten in short order. Sure, the bio may give an impression of credibility, but it is not until you provide real-time content that the audience's curiosity is satisfied, a challenge becomes demystified, or everyone's excitement is amplified. Only then do you actually prove your credibility to the audience.

Other tactics that are equally ineffective in establishing a speaker's credibility but that are also used for introducing speakers is giving highlights of the speaker's accomplishments or providing a litany of the speaker's professional and/or personal experiences. These are both problematic, too.

These three actions I am about to reveal to you, albeit unconventional, are necessary if you want to establish your credibility the right way and if you want to give the audience a different experience that will be unforgettable for all the right reasons. Whether you have an impressive background and bio or not, this is how you establish your credibility.

1. Forego having your bio read.

Audience members want to know how you will help them be more powerful, more productive, better professionals. They want to know how to be incredibly outstanding in all facets of their lives. You show your credibility by immediately demonstrating to the audience how well you know your subject matter and how well you are able to make it accessible to those listening to you. Furthermore, having a bio read shines the light on you rather than your audience, the importance of the audience, or your presentation topic. You should want people paying attention to your ideas, not you. Remember it matters not to the audience what *you* know or what you do until you show them how you help them with what *they* do![1]

2. Steer away from announcing too many of your accomplishments, doing so during inopportune moments, or announcing accomplishments with seemingly no point to doing so.

In select circles, it is what you do, especially if convened with fellow colleagues at an industry event. There are times when you have to toot your own horn! In other circles, particularly when making a presentation, it can appear braggadocios. This can alienate the audience, resulting in the impression you believe you are better than everyone assembled. While you may indeed have prominence, remaining humble goes a long way. Put the focus on your ideas and on the audience. Whether you have more accomplishments than you can count or if you are just getting started in your professional career and have work to do establishing yourself, this approach is a win-win. When you shine the light on everyone else in the room, *you* shine! When you make the other person feel like the most important person in the room, then *you* become the most important person in the room.

3. Take control of how you're introduced.

Arrive to the presentation room early and immediately ask the moderator to forego reading your bio. If she/he insists on reading one or saying *something* to introduce you, provide him/her with a one-liner: "Thank you for coming. Please welcome [insert your name]."

Or, do what the pros do, and that is to write and share with the organization and/or the moderator a brief introduction that has pizzazz. Here's an example of one I provide:

Have you ever experienced an energy that made you move to the edge of your seat or that made you stand to your feet? What about an excitement that stayed with you and had you talking about it long after an event ended? That is the best way to describe Bridgett McGowen, an award-winning author, an award-winning publisher, and an award-winning international professional speaker who is known to be both comical and memorable. She will not only energize you, but she will inspire you to not let anyone or anything get in the way of you being the most unforgettable person in the room. Today, Bridgett is here to share with you [insert presentation title].

But it doesn't always work out. The idea is by writing my own jazzed-up introduction, I put fire and energy behind my brand, but the challenge is it's truly written for my voice; plus, the amount of fire and energy is still going to be dependent upon the person reading it. You can offer to have the moderator practice it with you before the start of the presentation, but that depends on how comfortable both of you feel with that...

So, going forward...

a. Stop having your bio read before you present.

b. If some sort of introduction must be read, provide one you've written that aligns with the way you want to be introduced.

c. My personal favorite: Don't be afraid to ask the moderator to skip the bio or the introduction altogether so you can quickly begin to give the audience what it came to get.

---

[1]For more on how to properly introduce yourself, see "The One and Only Way to Ever Start Your Presentation" in chapter 3.

HOW YOU MUST VIEW YOURSELF AS A PRESENTER THIS MOMENT FORWARD

Negative views of yourself as a public speaker raise your anxiety and become a self-fulfilling prophecy. If you *think* you are awful, then trust me; there is a good chance you *will* be awful. If you *think* the audience is bored, then rest assured—the audience *will* be bored.

However, if you look at presenting as an opportunity to show how amazing you are, impart information, or get people excited, then the negative thoughts are scrapped.

Public speaking is only the vehicle, and it should not worry you. It furthers your reach, extends your voice, and positions you to grow in your profession. You do not engage in public speaking, but you engage in educating others. You engage in amazing audiences, delivering information, and transforming others. It is a paradigm shift required to establish your credibility.

REAL TALK PRINCIPLE

As you think, so you are. If you think positively about what you do, then you will perform positively. You will.

Start looking at your presentations this way: even if you know only 10 percent of what there is to know about a topic on which you are presenting, for the most part, that is inextricably more than what your audience knows about the topic. That right there should make your chest stick out at least an inch!

View yourself as the expert, and maintain this mindset before and throughout your presentation. Doing so will build you up. It will help reduce anxiety and lessen your worries about judgment. And another attitude to consider when working to diminish nerves and boost your confidence is this: if people want to be so judgmental, then they should get up in the front of the room and try to do what you are doing. (If you believe you detected a note of attitude there, you are spot-on. It takes courage to make a presentation. You do not need pressure from anyone who does not have good intentions.)

Those who are pros at presenting, who know the nerves and the strength it takes to be up there in front of a room, will be on your side; they will refrain from giving you a hard time. And as for those who are amateurs or who are completely unskilled at public speaking...do you really care what they have to say if it is not positive or constructive? (For this reason, endeavor to wait at least 48 hours before reviewing audience feedback. You want to revel for as long as possible in that magical feeling of having done a great job, and nothing will bring you down faster than one negative comment from an audience member that may be well-meaning but whose comments are simultaneously ego-deflating.)

Decide that you will become an expert on three to five specific points and identify them for your audience. If a participant tries to veer off in a direction outside of those three to five points, then refocus the group and remind everyone of your objectives and agenda. Emphasize your intention to keep the session on track. Saying something as simple as "That's a great/interesting/fascinating point. We are focusing on X today, so in the interest of staying on track, let's discuss that after the session."

Additionally, find an unexpected fact or recently released statistic relative to the topic and/or the audience that you later incorporate into your presentation. This is an effective way to surprise everyone, break the pattern of your presentation, or give a fresh point of view even to those who may be particularly well-versed in the topic.

Finally, if you know the audience will be filled with relevant experts beforehand, then consider enlisting the help of a co-presenter. Teaming up can make the experience more enjoyable for everyone, and it can feel less intimidating to you.

The audience is not hoping you stumble and fail. The audience is cheering, applauding, and hoping you will do an incredible job and that you will make a difference. Remember this. They want to see you shine, so that is precisely what you do. Get up there and shine.

REFLECT, REVIEW, AND RESPOND: DO YOU KNOW HOW TO ESTABLISH YOUR CREDIBILITY?

1. How effective is your introduction of yourself during your presentations? What do you need to change?

2. What kinds of body language establish your credibility?

3. In what ways does your attire mirror your message and your brand? What changes, if any, do you need to make?

4. What audience analyses do you need to conduct? How does this help establish your credibility?

5. What you do if you do not have an impressive résumé or a knockout background but you need to be seen as a credible speaker?

6. What view do you have of yourself as a public speaker? What changes, if any, should you make to that view?

Chapter 3

GIVE EVERYONE
A REASON TO LISTEN
TO YOU

Chapter 3

GIVE EVERYONE
A REASON TO LISTEN
TO YOU

To assume you have the power to compel people to listen to you, it requires more than you being the one on the stage with a lavalier mic clipped to your lapel. I learned this very early on when I started teaching in 2002; it wasn't enough that I was the instructor of record and that I had in my backpack the textbook with all the answers; I had to come with more if I expected young 18- and 19-year-old college freshmen minds to take an interest in college writing, especially at 7:00 a.m. on a Monday morning! I had to show up and give them a reason to listen to me.

But starting with a joke was not going to get the job done. That's what other experts will suggest you should do.

Telling stories is nice, and they bode well for creating that mental hook, but is it feasible to have a story for the start of every presentation? Startling statistics, interesting graphics, and arresting photography are great options, too, but they don't do the trick when it comes to giving everyone a reason to listen.

They do not add value to your presentation, especially if you are presenting to busy professionals. So, you are back at square one, wondering how to start your presentation in a way that will immediately make everyone lean in.

In this chapter, you will know how to...

- start your presentation in a way that reduces (or completely eliminates) the blank, uninterested stares from your audience

- maximize the start of your presentation so all eyes and all ears are on you from the first moment you speak until the last

- get your audience engaged before anyone even shows up for your presentation

- engage audiences in ways that further your objectives, that are meaningful to listeners, and that work no matter your presentation topic

- appeal to all the ways people like to process information

- avoid having an activity just for the sake of having an activity

- engage your audience without you or your audience feeling silly

THE HUGE MISTAKE PRESENTERS MAKE AND HOW TO AVOID IT

Common questions presenters ask themselves before making presentations are ...

"I have so much information to cover until I don't know where to start. What do I do?!"

"My presentations are pretty good, but what can I do to make them great?!"

"What can I say to make my audiences like me?!"

However, none of these questions matter if you do not ask and answer this one: "What do I want my audience to know or to be able to do by the time I finish my presentation?" Before you make another presentation, you must ask and answer that question, then the next step is for your content to deliver. With this approach, you reverse-engineer your presentation, starting with the end in mind. This means you first identify what they need to walk away with by the end of your session, the most important part of your planning, then you identify the three to five concepts you need to teach or tell them that will make that happen.

So many presentations omit this step, and it is a colossal misstep. *Colossal!* They do not answer this question, leading audiences down roads of annoyance and absolute presentation boredom.

They sit there, politely waiting for the end, gaining little inspiration or insight. Furthermore, the failure to answer that question results in presentations being little more than information dumps, which, of course, is oftentimes quite disappointing for listeners. Thought must go into what you will present, how it will be presented, and what everyone will get out of your presentation; work to have an intentional plan not just for your presentation but for how everyone will benefit from listening to you. Do not just get up and talk.

To just get up and talk is not sexy.

That's the missing link and the huge mistake so many presenters make—they oftentimes just throw information at the audience without first asking "What does the audience want?" or "What does the audience really need?"

To avoid this mistake, here is the three-part process to forever change how you approach your presentations going forward:

1. Think about what you know and all the information you have relative to your presentation topic. Ask yourself "What do I know? What do I have to offer everyone?"

2. Think about all the questions, issues, and challenges your audience has as they relate to your topic. In short, ask yourself "What are they coming to get? What do they want from me? What do they need?"

3. Finally, take what you know to give them what they want. Take what you have to give them what they need.

The goal is to put people in a better position after having heard you. Ask yourself what you want to accomplish because you should want to do more than just talk and get it over with. You should endeavor to create ah-ha moments, turn on light bulbs, spark creativity, excite people, and make everyone think of new possibilities. To do so, you must create a presentation that has real purpose. Do not view presenting as a mere box that needs to be checked off. Again, ask yourself "What do I want my audience to know or to do after I finish my presentation?"

Here are the three steps you take to smoothly make your way through preparing for your presentations with determination, excitement, passion, enthusiasm, and purpose so you are not merely offering your audience the dreaded information dump.

1. Decide exactly how you will excite everyone.

Your listeners do not need sleep; they need their heart rates to increase. Do this by giving them the benefits of the presentation—what will they gain by listening to you—and why the presentation has significance for them. In short, why should they care? Seriously. What is going to make their eyebrows go up? What is going to put them on the edges of their seats? This is intricately connected to the act of informing listeners. Recall the number one reason adults will listen to you. They listen because they know *why* they should listen. There is a sense of excitement when you realize you can enhance yourself, your performance, or your potential as a result of having done X. Get your audiences to crave what you have to share with them! If you convey how an aspect of your listeners' lives or work will be better as a result of having spent their time engaged with you and your content during a presentation, then listeners cannot help but to bubble with excitement. Answer these three questions in every single presentation:

1. What is it?
2. How does it work?
3. Why does it matter?

What

Give a definition, explanation, detailed analysis of the topic. Tell them what it is as well as what it is not. Give them exactly what you would want to know if you knew absolutely nothing about the topic.

Using presentation skills as our sample topic, the WHAT I'd share with the audience is those skills are a set of tools you use to ensure that when you present, your presentation is indeed a communication tool that inspires, teaches, and motivates others to action. The skills can be used in both formal and informal environments. They can be used in one-to-one settings because everything you say should be a presentation, or they can (and should) be used in one-to-many settings.

How

Talk about its inner workings, its parts, who uses it, where it's used, in what instances one would use it, and how it fits into a community. Tell them the purpose it serves—that it's not just an idea but that it has utility.

Returning to our sample topic, the HOW is the skills are used by all kinds of professionals in all kinds of industries. The skills are meant to carefully combine information, graphics/images, and conversations so they come together in a fashion that gets people engaging in content in a meaningful way.

Why

This is where you give them a reason to listen. Explain what makes it stand out, what's its value, and what it helps them accomplish. Tell them WHY it's important—ostensibly, WHY they should bother to listen to you.

Finally—back to our example—effective presentation skills are important because if you want to be seen and you want to be heard, if you want to get rid of the jitters, if you want to be regarded as a credible individual, then you must pay careful attention to what you say and how you say it. Having a clear and organized plan as well as proven strategies for delivering a presentation is what will set you apart and have your listeners sitting up and taking notice of you and your ideas.

2. Draw them in with your excitement.

Capture and hold fast listeners' attention with your passion. Give your honest reaction to the content. Show that you love it. Find a way to love it if need be! Pull your audience into your world. Make everyone feel what you are feeling so there is no way anyone's attention will get diverted from what is occurring at the front of that room.

3. Make it a two-way street.

Get listeners immediately talking, writing, and/or moving so they know your voice, ideas, and actions are not the only valid ones in the room. Audience members learn more, lean in more, and are better inclined to act as you want them to act if the ideas appear to come from them. Did you catch that? If they are involved … if the presentation is a two-way street … if their voices are heard, then they are more likely to get on your bandwagon and pick up what you are putting down.

Sure, this takes conscious thought and preparation, but there is always this alternative: walk in, say "hello," then painfully subject your audience to 15, 30, or even 60 or more minutes of a sit-and-get, uninspired session. For which do you want to be remembered?

> Being a memorable speaker is second only to being a memorable person. Get a year's worth of habits to make you stand out in *Show Up and Show Out: 52 Communication Habits to Make You Even More Unforgettable.*

HOW TO GRAB YOUR AUDIENCE'S ATTENTION NO MATTER YOUR TOPIC

Avoid simply regurgitating information, and do not wait until the end of the presentation to solve a mystery or give a solution. Do not make an attempt to build up to a climax when you present, especially when addressing busy professionals. That does not get everyone's attention. On the opposite end of the spectrum, avoid checking the boxes or phoning it in.

REAL TALK PRINCIPLE

You grab and maintain audience attention
by immediately solving a mystery.

Give the audience members what they need in your opening words. Provide utility. The truth is you want to be able to hear a pin drop at this moment. When you know what your audience members' goals and needs are and you know how your words connect with those goals and needs, you have people listening closely.

Each audience member will have any one or any combination of these attitudes in your presentation. There will be those present who want you to ...

1. Cut to the chase; just give me the facts—nothing more nothing less, and at all costs, do not waste my time.

2. Establish a personal connection with me; make me feel like you get me, that you totally understand my point of view and my challenges.

3. Do not dare try to pull a fast one on me with information that does not align with what I already know to be true; I can smell foolishness from a mile away.

4. Bring the sizzle because I can sit at home and watch paint dry. I need you to show up with the excitement and the enthusiasm. Look and sound like you want to be here.

If you are suddenly forming an image of Aristotle in your mind, then you are on the right track. With the exception of number 4 (possibly because Aristotle would likely have never said "sizzle"), all of these attitudes are reminiscent of ethos, pathos, and logos—terms coined by Aristotle to identify the modes of persuasion. Here's your quick review of those little gems: Ethos is an ethical appeal meant to convince an audience of your credibility or character. Pathos is an emotional appeal meant to persuade an audience by appealing to the emotions. Logos is the appeal to an audience through reason.

To speak to these four attitudes, in a very short amount of time, you must use the 4P's of Engagement: pull in your audience, pump up your audience, pass the mic to your audience, and provide the audience with content.

You PULL THEM IN by creating a connection and a sense of rapport.

You PUMP THEM UP and get them excited by driving an enthusiasm for what is to come, by giving the session objectives, and by moving them to say "Yes, this is going to be worth my time!"

You PASS THE MIC by making the presentation about the audience members and including them in the conversation.

Finally, you PROVIDE THE CONTENT by giving the agenda—which details how you will arrive at the objectives—and your power introduction; then deliver the content of your presentation, the objective material you plan to cover.[1]

Avoid waiting until the end of the presentation to pull a trick out of a hat, to solve a mystery, or to give a solution. Immediately give them a reason to listen to you, high-five a neighbor, and say "Oh yeah! This is gonna be a good one!"

---

[1]For more on the power introduction, see "The Way You Have Been Introducing Yourself to Your Audience is All Wrong" in chapter 2, and for more on the 4Ps of Engagement, see "The One and Only Way to Ever Start Your Presentation" in chapter 3.

THE ONE AND ONLY WAY TO EVER START YOUR PRESENTATION

If I started a presentation like this, there is nothing there that tells you why you should listen to me:

Good day.

It's great to see everyone.

Today, we will cover presentation skills.

Let's get started.

However, if I started like this, you know why you should bother to listen to me:

Do you believe everyone can make a great presentation? When you hear the word "presentation," some of you may cringe. Others may think "There is nothing to this!" Either way, you are likely to automatically think in terms of good presentations and bad presentations.

By the end of this session, you will know how to start, deliver, and close your presentations with a bang, but most importantly, you will know how to keep your cool the entire time you are presenting so you look and feel like the powerhouse that you are!

Specifically, you will know how to give everyone a reason to listen to you, you will know how to engage audiences in meaningful ways without feeling silly, you'll know the question you should never ask your audience, and you will have a three-part process that will forever change how you deliver presentations.

My name is Bridgett McGowen, and what I do is I help professionals be the most engaging, dynamic, incredible communicators ever.

The opening of this session sounds far more interesting because it takes into account the audience's past, present, and future.

To focus on the past, ask yourself where your audience was relative to your topic before they entered your presentation.

From what mental situation were they coming that led them to your presentation? What were they thinking? What do they need? What do they want from the message you are about to deliver?

I focused on the past here: Do you believe everyone can make a great presentation? When you hear the word "presentation," some of you may cringe. Others may think "There is nothing to this!" Either way, you are likely to automatically think in terms of good presentations and bad presentations.

Transition to the present.

How will you address their situation with the presentation you are about to deliver? How will you speak to what they are thinking? How will you give them what they need or want? What information will you provide? What will you do right now?

I transitioned to the present here: Specifically, you will know how to give everyone a reason to listen to you, you will know how to engage audiences in meaningful ways without feeling silly, you'll know the question you should never ask your audience, and you will have a three-part process that will forever change how you deliver presentations.

Look to the future.

Clarify how everyone's future will look as a result of engaging in your presentation.

Where will they be after your presentation? What will they be able to do after your presentation? What is the overall solution they will have after listening to you? Future-pace them. Get them to see the finished product and get excited about the finished product.

I looked to the future here: By the end of this session, you will know how to start, deliver, and close your presentations with a bang. More importantly, you will know how to keep your cool the entire time you are presenting so you look and feel like the powerhouse that you are!

The opening of this session sounds far more interesting also because not only does it speak to the past, present, and future, but it also speaks to everyone, using the 4P's of Engagement: pull in your audience, pump up your audience, pass the mic to your audience, and provide the audience with content.

Pull them in (create a connection and a sense of rapport): *Do you believe everyone can make a great presentation? When you hear the word "presentation," some of you may cringe. Others may think "There is nothing to this!" Either way, it is likely you automatically think in terms of good presentations and bad presentations.*

Pump them up (excite and drive an enthusiasm for what is to come): *By the end of this session, you will know the different ways to start your presentations with a bang, but most importantly, you will know how to keep your cool the entire time you are presenting so you look and feel like the powerhouse that you are!*

Pass the mic (make the presentation about the audience members): Use "you" references at least four times; avoid using first person point of view (I, me, my) as much as possible. (The example I provide has seventeen "you" references. Go back and count them. Go on. I'll hold your spot in the book while you count.) While "we" sounds nice and collaborative, the reality is it is what the audience will get out of the presentation that is the main priority, not what you and the audience (we) will get out of it. Your presentation is about what the audience will be able to do, not what you will do together. Make sure in your opening words that your use of "you" is not accusatory in terms of "You need to do X" or "You should do Y." The use of it needs to be in an inspirational and aspirational sense during your power intro such as "You have been wanting X" or "You have been wondering about Y." It should come from a point of view that signals to the listeners you understand their needs and desires.

It's at this moment you are working to continue to build rapport with your listeners. And remember to be careful that you do not place unnecessary emphasis on your "you" references when you speak them. I've heard people do this when trying this technique for the first time. Simply say "you" the same way you would say it any other time.

Provide the content (give the agenda and your power introduction): *Specifically, you will know how to give everyone a reason to listen to you, you will know how to engage audiences in meaningful ways without feeling silly, you'll know the question you should never ask your audience, and you will have a three-part process that will forever change how you deliver presentations. My name is Bridgett McGowen, and what I do is I help professionals be the most engaging, dynamic, incredible communicators ever.*[1]

Here is an example you might use this in a corporate presentation:

Pull them in: Your company boasts quite an impressive set of numbers. More than half of your employees have worked for Fortune 500 companies, and you have an remarkable new customer acquisition rate. You want to ensure you do everything you can to maximize your team members' efforts and ensure you retain your customers.

Pump them up: By the end of this session, you will know how BMcTALKS can help your team engage in more productive communication that also positively impacts customer retention rates.

The key to pulling in audience members is to find out what they have and to understand what they want via an audience analysis.[2] Then to pump them up, demonstrate what you have that will give the audience what it wants or needs.

To organize your presentation in a manner that will immediately grab the audience's attention and shed light on why everyone should listen to you, start with this:

Clarify why they should listen. This is where you state the objectives. Identify what everyone will know or be able to do upon conclusion of the presentation. This is the unspoken expectation all audiences have. This means you clarify how your presentation, product, or topic connects to the last presentation or meeting. Draw parallels between your presentation and the work everyone does. Explain how this one puzzle piece (your presentation) fits with the larger picture; clearly illustrate how your session will contribute to moving listeners closer to fulfilling their personal or professional goals. Let them know what new knowledge or abilities they will have by the time the presentation comes to an end—knowledge or abilities that they did not have before listening to you speak. That is your starting point. This is where the audience realizes *why* everyone should care.

Next, create your agenda items that clearly demonstrate WHAT you will cover and HOW time will be spent. This is how you create an intentional plan for executing your presentation or your roadmap. The agenda is your plan for delivering on your three to five objectives. Use this as a roadmap to navigate your way through your presentation.

Finally, provide your power introduction that clarifies what you do that connects to what the audience does. Remember—a power introduction does not involve establishing your credibility by covering your biography or having it read by someone.[1]

Constantly focus on why your audience should listen. It is because you know how to help ... because you understand ... because you will offer solutions. Bear in mind you do not have to feel like you must offer solutions to bleeding-from-the-neck problems. If you are positioned to contribute to making the endeavors of a person's life or profession more easily attainable in any way, then you have a winner. Always think: "What do I do that makes my audience better?" When you take this approach, this automatically excites the audience to want to hear everything you have to say.

---

[1] For information and details on how to create your power introduction, see "The Way You Have Been Introducing Yourself to Your Audience is All Wrong" in chapter 2 and "The Only Presentation Plan You Will Ever Need Part 2: The Actual Presentation" in chapter 4.

[2] For more on conducting an audience analysis, see "How Well Do You Really Know Your Audience?" in chapter 2.

WHY NO ONE LAUGHS WHEN YOU CRACK A JOKE AND WHAT TO DO INSTEAD

Have you ever seen (or given) a presentation that started with a joke that went horribly wrong or where the most unfortunate happened—no one laughed at the joke? Did you chalk it up as the person simply not being funny? That's possible, but I will tell you precisely what happened as well as how to avoid this dilemma.

The joke flopped because at the time it was told, at the start of the presentation, the audience had received no value and the audience was not connected to the presenter. As such, the presenter had not given the audience a reason to laugh. The joke in itself was not enough to form a connection, and if the audience has not warmed up to you, has not received any reason to like you, has gained no value yet from listening to you, then there is nothing funny you can say at the outset. Nothing.

When you give the audience a reason to listen to you, they will find value in you, they will connect with you, they will warm up to you, and they will easily find a reason to like you and subsequently laugh at your jokes even if they aren't funny. With every idea you communicate, you want to connect with your audience and give everyone a reason to shake her or his head and think, "Oh yes. This is gonna be a good one!" This is the response for which you should always aim. Once you demonstrate value in your presentation's content, then you are positioned to crack a joke. And again, even if it is not funny, people will laugh; but this happens only after you establish your credibility and give everyone a reason to listen.

> ## REAL TALK PRINCIPLE
>
> If you give your audience a reason to listen to you, then you can tell the lamest joke in the world, and because you have immediately given them value, people will laugh.

Humor is an absolute plus in a presentation. When we laugh, according to Naomi Bagdonas, co-author of *Humor, Seriously: Why Humor is a Secret Weapon in Business and Life*, "our brains release the hormone oxytocin, and we're essentially cued to form an emotional bond with [the] person [who made you laugh]."

If you make the decision to add a moment of levity to your presentation, then these four P's of incorporating humor—personality, purposeful, practice, and point—are a must.

Personality

You are not a comedian. Furthermore, it may not even be part of your personality to be funny. Or if you *do* have a funny personality, then we are back at square one in that you are not a professional comedian. Even the most celebrated professional comedians will tell you successful joke-telling takes a lot of work. It involves writing, rewriting, editing, or even hiring a team of writers.

When in search of ways to add levity, learn from those comedians who make you laugh and the ways you personally make others laugh. Observe the structure, style, construction, and pacing of a favorite comedian, paying careful attention to not just what the comedian says but also how it's said—the nuances of the language. Second, identify things you already do that make others laugh. This one is my preference because it's authentically you and takes very little practice. Everyone has the ability to make others laugh. While it may be a rare occurrence, there are those people or situations that bring out your inner comedian. Think back to what you do in those instances and ask yourself how you can weave it into your speaking. With friends, my funniest moments are when I use hyperbolic language, self-deprecation, and plays on words, so I add those to my presentations.

Purposeful

The intended purpose of your presentation is not likely to entertain, and the audience does not show up expecting that. They came for real information. However, if you want to add humor, do so in a purposeful way with relevant news items, anecdotes, court rulings, and industry magazines, and riff off those. Crack a joke about the impossibility or outrageousness of the findings or reporting in those references.

Practice

If you do opt to add a joke to your presentation, then try it out on colleagues, friends, or family first to ensure it is indeed funny.

However, if you tell a joke and it flops, move on. Do not try to explain it—doing so only makes it worse.

Point

Ask yourself why you want to add a joke in the first place. Are you using it as a diversion? Do you want to distract the audience from yourself or the substance of your presentation? If so, then what is your point in doing that? Or do you just want to see smiles in the audience to gain a sense of approval?

Here is how to ensure your own likability whether you prompt smiles or not: Give your listeners what they came to get. At the start of your presentation, give them what you promised you would give them. And, here is the bonus: When you do that, and if you tell even the lamest joke on the planet, it will result in laughter. They will laugh because they believe in your message. In other words, they are feeling you. You have likely seen audiences laugh at a presenter's corny joke, and you think "Really? REALLY?!" Here's what happened: They laughed because they were feeling the presenter. When the audience is feeling you, they will connect with you. They will like you. And when they like you, smiles and laughter will naturally occur.

STOP RAMBLING. IT'S NOT CUTE.

There is so much you want to cover and only so much time to do it. Subconsciously, you want your audience to fall as deeply in love with your topic as possible. This tends to cause a problem.

There is nothing wrong with wanting your audience to find the same value in your content as you find in it. The challenge lies in this desire propelling you to share and share and share to the point that you end up rambling, rambling, and rambling. By going off on long-winded tangents or regularly losing your train of thought, you also lose your effectiveness, and you diminish your power to communicate.[1]

First, keep in mind that you are not there to create experts out of your listeners. Would it be awesome if you could? Absolutely! Is that realistic in the course of one presentation? Absolutely not.

Think of the number of hours, days, weeks, months—even years or decades—it took you to acquire the degree of knowledge you have on your presentation topic. As such, remember the time you have to present is limited; hence, the material you provide must be limited in quantity but not—you guessed it—quality. To avoid rambling—or to at least keep it to a minimum—give your audience the three biggest components that will spark curiosity, then give just enough information to shed light on why you are so passionate and/or why the components are so important.

Second, with those three big components, remember who is in your audience. Ask yourself …

1. What does everyone need to hear? What is the main takeaway?

2. How do I want them to react to the information? How will their beliefs and actions be changed?

3. Why does the information matter? Why should this be important to everyone?

Next, stop and listen to how much you are talking. If you have been talking for more than 10 to 15 minutes without getting input from the audience (or if you have a shorter presentation, then you will need to talk for less than 10 minutes before getting audience input), then you have been talking too much. You may have even been rambling as a result. Provide opportunities for the audience to chime in.[2] Doing so will ensure that the sound of your voice is not the only one filling the space. Additionally, strategically incorporate pauses into your message.[3] Not only is your message more digestible for the audience when you do this, but it also forces you to slow down and hear just how much you are speaking.

Finally, always be aware of the audience. Pay attention to their body language. Do you see the glazed doughnut look? Is the audience mentally or even physically checking out by look-ing at watches, shifting in seats, thumbing through the hand-out you gave, engaging with devices, or taking part in sidebar conversations? All of these are telltale signs that you are causing the audience to become disengaged, and rambling may be the culprit. When this occurs, the audience is no longer interested in what you have to say. The easiest way to turn this around is to shift gears and get the audience engaging with the content, giving you time to regroup.[2]

---

[1]For strategies to support you when you lose your train of thought, see "What to Do if You Lose Your Train of Thought" in chapter 1.

[2]For ideas on how to get audience input and to get everyone engaged with your content, see "Why No One Responses When You Ask 'Are There Any Questions?' And What to Ask Instead" in chapter 3.

[3]For more on how to incorporate pauses into your message, see "The Power of the Pause: 9 Types of Pauses You Need to Add to Your Presentations" in chapter 3.

THE POWER OF THE PAUSE: 9 TYPES OF PAUSES YOU NEED TO ADD TO YOUR PRESENTATIONS

A pause can achieve a variety of effects in your presentation and is one of the secrets of the most skilled presenters. Aside from forcing you to slow down your speech, it can make your presentation even more effective depending on the type of pause you use and when you use it. Here are nine pauses you should incorporate into your presentations to make them more interesting and to make you a more powerful speaker.

1. Comma Pause

The comma pause, which lasts one to two seconds, is pretty much what it sounds like. It's a pause you insert roughly where you would see a comma in writing, but it occurs approximately twice as often in your speech. With written material, one can always return to the text and reread it to confirm an understanding of the content. But this is not possible in speaking. Using the comma pause—grouping words into shorter sentences and phrases so the audience can follow what you're saying—gives your audience time to process.

2. End-of-Thought Pause

Similar to the comma pause, the end-of-thought pause is where a period would be in writing, separating one thought from another. Oftentimes, speakers' presentations are filled with run-ons and fused sentences. The one- to two-second end-of-thought pause gives audiences the necessary time to process content, especially if it is unusual, emotional, poetic, dramatic, or new.

3. Highlight Pause

Use the highlight pause to set up what is coming next. For example, "Do you know what happened ...?" *pause* This pause gets the audience's attention, heightens interest, and gets the everyone to lean in. The rest of the three- to seven-second highlight pause requires you follow-up with a statement that incentivizes your audience for following along with you.

4. Thinking Pause

A thinking pause gives your audience time to well ... think! A three- to seven-second thinking pause is particularly important when you provide complex or unusual statements. This type of pause says to your audience "This is important, so ensure you take a moment to reflect on it," or "I'm providing space for you to think."

5. Effect Pause

An effect pause lasts one to two seconds where you let words hang in the air, creating a feeling that something interesting, exciting, or surprising is about to happen—that a shift is on the horizon.

6. Impromptu Pause

The one- to two-second impromptu pause creates a feeling of spontaneity, and it keeps your audience interested. It suggests you are thinking about your words as you speak and that you are not simply regurgitating a script you have delivered several times before.

7. Control Pause

This pause is particularly useful during a Q&A segment. Give a succinct response to the question, pause, then ask "Does that answer your question?"[1]

8. Sensory Pause

The sensory pause allows the audience to hear, smell, see, and feel what you are describing. For example, "Imagine it" *pause* "July" *pause* "The San Diego convention center" *pause* "The voices of conference-goers ignite an energy in you" *pause* "But as you confidently stroll through the exhibit hall, you suddenly stop in your tracks" *pause* "You read a name on a name badge that is strangely familiar" *pause* "Your palms grow sweaty" *pause* "Your mind races" *pause* "Your heart rate speeds up" "This is an encounter for which you never prepared, but now" *pause* "It's go time!"

9. Variety Pause

Audiences have short attention spans, so it's necessary to add variety to your presentation and to orchestrate your message. Avoid the same tone, the same pace, the same energy level, the same gestures, and the same movements for too long. Using a variety pause aids in getting rid of sameness, and it simultaneously keeps everyone's attention longer. Use variety pauses to delineate key points and to break audience boredom.

---

[1] For more on how to expertly handle questions, see "The 7-Step Method to Expertly Answer Any Question" in chapter 5.

AUDIENCE ENGAGEMENT DONE RIGHT

You have attended those presentations where the speaker had a lot of games and props and bells and whistles. Or they had you standing and moving and clapping and so on. (That may have been one of my presentations!) Do not get me wrong; there is nothing inherently problematic with this, especially if masterfully done.

At the same time, you must be incredibly careful with this type of engagement as you will create two schools of thought amongst audience members: either they love it or they loathe it. Always be aware there are presenters who can pull off what seems like the impossible with activities designed to foster audience engagement. Just because they may have everyone in the audience turning cartwheels does not mean that you, too, can do the same and achieve similar levels of engagement. Your attempt could turn into an epic fail for one reason or another, especially if your interactions are too lively or if the audience is not receptive to such activity. You most definitely run the risk of losing, turning off, or offending members of your audience.

However, if you only cover content and do not engage the audience, then you create a boring experience for everyone. Presenters often realize this, so they will incorporate a few "Are there any question?" moments, which does not work.[1] Or they will go in search of activities and games. Stop right there. Step away from the "activities for my presentation" Google search. Get your hand off that mouse. Now.

What these game-seekers fail to realize is this: adding an activity to a presentation is not the correct starting point for audience engagement. I understand you do not want the audience to just sit and listen to you. I get it. And you are to be applauded for recognizing this and wanting to make adjustments. But just finding an activity so the audience has "something to do" is not the answer.

Audience engagement done right means you start with designing great questions that will fuel conversations, inspire action, lead to additional questions, and help everyone envision the future. However, if you start with the activity without putting conscious thought into the question(s) that serves as the basis for the activity, then that is when you have challenges with engagement. Audience engagement done right means you first decide on the great questions you will ask your audience, then and only then are you empowered to facilitate virtually any game or activity with great success.[1]

---

[1] Find out why asking "Are there any questions?" does not work as well as how to design great questions in "Why No One Responds When You Ask 'Are There Any Questions?' And What to Ask Instead" in chapter 3.

WHY NO ONE RESPONDS WHEN YOU ASK "ARE THERE ANY QUESTIONS?" AND WHAT TO ASK INSTEAD

No one responds to "Are there any questions?" because it is not a question that is designed in a way that motivates a modern-day audience to provide a response. In the spirit of keeping it real, the question is boring. It is expected. It is nothing new. Everyone has heard it a million times, so it has gotten to a point now where people usually sit quietly, waiting for someone else to do the work necessary to answer the question, and trust me—there is work involved with responding to this question! However, presenters keep asking "Are there any questions?" 1) because it is easy, or 2) because it is what they have always done or what they have always seen other presenters do, or 3) because they want to ensure their message is understood by everyone, but they do not know anything better to ask instead that will help them ascertain if everyone was really picking up what they were putting down. It's time to change that.

REAL TALK PRINCIPLE

Never ask "Are there any questions?" Never.

Whether you ask "Are there any questions?" in an attempt to engage your audience or as a means for concluding your presentation, if you continue to pose this query, then you will continue to get crickets. (An alternative to "Are there any questions?" is "What questions do you have?" Don't use that one either for all the reasons I'm about to give you.)

The reason you get crickets is not necessarily because you have done such an outstanding job comprehensively delivering your topic until everyone fully understands and there *are* no questions. It's because the question is too hard to answer, and it does not sufficiently guide the audience to think. Recall I indicated there is work involved with answering "Are there any questions?" If expected to provide an answer to that query, members must silently and quickly do any combination of the following:

1. Think back to the specific piece of content you presented about which they have a question.

2. Ensure they use the same jargon, wording, or phrasing you used so they do not run the risk of feeling or looking silly because they did not have the language quite right.

3. Recall what about that piece of content was unclear or troubling.

4. Form the query.

5. Assess if that is the "right" question and whether it gets at the heart of what they want to ask. If not, then they must revise the question.

Only after all of that has taken place, does one feel relatively ready to verbalize a question. That is work!

If you want to check for understanding, instead of asking "Are there any questions?" and continuing to get the silent stares, do this:

1. Conduct a recap of what you just covered. This is done by simply stating, "We just covered A, B, and C."
2. Then, ask "Which of these is still unclear to you?"

Easy, right?

This way, it reminds everyone of what you just covered, and it focuses everyone. And if you get someone who says clarity is needed on point B, then there you have it. Do not ask "What don't you understand?" or "What's unclear to you?" Break it down to its simplest form, explaining what it is (and what it's not), how it works, and why it's important.

And to arrive at more effective questions that people will actually answer because the question has them adding to their knowledge base what you just presented, paint a picture of the stakes, have the audience apply the information, then have everyone do the work.

Paint a Picture

First, you paint a picture of the stakes by asking yourself the following as each query relates to your presentation topic with X, Y, and Z being your presentation objectives:

1. What will happen if audience members do not know about X?

2. What will happen if the audience members do not master/understand/embrace Y?

3. How will audience members be negatively or positively impacted because of Z?

4. What outcomes do the listeners want? What outcomes do I want for my listeners? And how will the information I provide get everyone there?

Apply the Information

Now that you know what is at stake for your audience, what they risk by not knowing or not understanding as a result of you failing to ask better questions, use that information as the foundation for formulating better questions that can then be used in any activity.

If you want to get them to get EXCITED about the content, ask...

1. What do you like about X?

2. [Based on what I just presented], what is it you cannot wait to do/try/attend? Explain.

3. What caught your attention/surprised you about X?

4. What is your favorite part about X?

5. What will your team like most about X?

If you want the audience to CHANGE A CURRENT BEHAVIOR, ask...

1. Based on Y, what will you do differently?

2. What will you say differently?

3. In what ways will you use Y in your life? Work? Family?

4. Based on Y, what changes will you see with X?

5. How do you think Y will be better if you change X?

If you want them to take the information you provided and APPLY it to a specific area of their businesses, professions, or interests, ask...

1. How do you see yourself using Z? List three instances.

2. How will this improve/positively impact X, Y, or Z?

3. What's a current challenge that Z will help solve?

If you want them to THINK BIG PICTURE or to PLAN FOR THE FUTURE, ask...

1. What does this information mean for X?

2. Out of these features/products/events, which one, two, or three will you highlight, use, or attend? Why?

3. Now that you know X, what you be able to do in the future that you cannot do now?

An important note here is ensure you design your questions so the audience consistently thinks in positive terms. Avoid asking questions such as "What do you not like about X?" or "What is the worst part of Y?" These questions have the propensity to work well if you want to take the temperature of the room early in your presentation and to create an awareness of a problem for which your presentation will provide solutions; however, I will still advise against it because it prompts the audience to have negative thoughts.

If you are short on time and you simply want to ask a question (without prompting the audience to talk with a colleague, write, listen, or move[1]), you must practice the ABCs of asking questions. This is a technique where you ask a great question; breathe while you silently count to seven in your head, providing them thinking time; then call on a participant. Refrain from asking a question and immediately expecting a response because ... well ... it is not going to happen.

When you ask a participant a question, especially in a group setting, remember the listener must mentally perform a number of actions. Consider this. If I asked you what you had for dinner yesterday, you would have to stop and think for a second. The questions you ask in your presentations are more involved than that one, so you can imagine the audience will need more time to answer. Again, remember the ABCs of asking questions—ask a great question, breathe while you silently count to seven in your head, then call on a participant for an answer.

Do the Work

Finally, have the audience do the work: prompt them to talk, write, listen, or move.[1]

In short, to create engagement or to check for understanding, do not ask "Are there any questions?" or "What questions do you have?" Doing so will only elicit silence. Audience engagement done right means asking great questions—a secret used by all the pros. If you paint a picture of the stakes, then audience engagement will come naturally. In other words, powerful audience engagement is not dependent upon an activity; it is dependent upon asking powerful questions.

---

[1] For ideas on how to get participants talking, writing, listening to each other, and moving, see "How to Ensure You Reach Everyone in the Room" in chapter 3.

HOW TO ENSURE YOU REACH
EVERYONE IN THE ROOM

After you paint a picture of the stakes where you clearly outline what is at risk and, therefore, what everyone needs to understand and after you've had the audience apply the information you provided via a great set of open-ended questions, decide how you want the audience to respond—how you want them to do the work.[1]

Consider the four communication and learning preferences of your audience members: VARK. There will be people present who want to receive and deliver information visually (V), others who have an auditory (A) preference, those with a read/write (R) partiality, and those who prefer kinesthetic (K) inputs and outputs.

To ensure you attend to all preferences during the course of your presentation, have the audience view content, discuss and listen, read and/or write, and move.

Visual: Provide supporting resources so your audience is not just listening to you. Have a slide deck for everyone to view in conjunction with your talk or a handout for them to follow along with or to reference after your presentation.

Auditory: You have the auditory piece covered by the mere virtue of your speaking; however, to do more, after delivering 10 to

15 minutes of content, pose a question, then say "Turn to your neighbor, and discuss for X minute(s), then prepare to share with the larger group."

Read/Write: Provide content for them to read then discuss, giving these directions: "Pair with a college where one colleague speaks for 30 seconds while you listen and take notes without speaking, then switch." You can also have the audience engage in a one-minute paper.[2]

Kinesthetic: To get them moving, pose a question or, in the case of number 2 below, a provocative statement, then say any one of these …

1. "Think of your answer, and prepare to stand and shout it out."

2. "Stand. Move to the left side of the room if you strongly agree with the statement, or move to the right side if you strongly disagree with the statement. Be prepared to defend your position."

3. Go for a three-minute walk with a colleague and discuss your answers to the question. (When the three minutes are up, ring a bell once or use another non-overly-intrusive noise-maker to indicate they are to return to their seats.)

This way, you appeal to the different ways people like to process information: visually, auditorily, in written form, or kinesthetically.

Again, once you have great questions, you can take any activity from any source and use it to engage you audience.[1] But start with the question first. When you design questions by first painting a picture of the stakes and focusing on how you will have everyone apply the information and do the work, you put yourself in a position to confidently insert virtually any activity into your presentation.

----

[1] For more on painting a picture of the stakes and designing great questions, see "Why No One Responds When You Ask 'Are There Any Questions?' And What to Ask Instead" in chapter 3.

[2] See more on the one-minute paper in "Move Them From Passive to Active: 3 Really Easy Audience Engagement Tools" in chapter 3.

CREATE ENGAGEMENT BEFORE YOU SAY A WORD: 20+ STRATEGIES FOR GENERATING GREAT PRESENTATION TITLES

Audience engagement begins before you even speak a word. It begins with the title of your session. People will attend a presentation if it appears to show a good promise of bringing about benefits or solving immediate problems. So, to do this, provide a title for your presentation that gives the impression that this simply cannot wait!

You want to make your presentation sound so red-hot and delicious that missing it would be downright criminal. This begins by titling your presentation in a way that makes everyone say, "Let me get out the pen, paper, and popcorn because this is going to be a good one!"

On its own, though, a catchy title is not an automatic guarantee a presentation will be great. As you know, the second part of the equation is your content must deliver on the promise your title makes. Plus, keep in mind that a snappy title is not an absolute requirement for every session you deliver; however, it sure does give you some mileage when trying to catch an audience's attention!

To create attention-getting titles for your sessions, consider the following principles that companies use to create their own unforgettable slogans:

1. Identification. A good title remains consistent with and/or identifies one or more of the hallmarks you are trying to convey either by obviously stating it/them or by strong implication.

2. Memorable. Titles should catch an audience's attention and contain a phrase that is relatively easy for people to remember. If they are able to recall the title after the session has come to a close, then that is even better!

3. Beneficial. Reveal your purpose and what the audience will receive or learn by attending the session; create a positive feeling.

4. Simple. Use short, power words whenever possible.[1]

Number 1 is key for speakers who want to ensure they consistently stay on brand. For instance, I tend to use "sizzle" and "blazing-hot" quite frequently in my session titles; you will see the same from other speakers where they will incorporate words or acronyms that align with their messaging or brand. Number 1 is optional, but 2, 3, and 4 are key to creating great titles.

Consider having two parts to your title—a short hook followed by a colon, hyphen, or ellipses plus the bait, which specifies what people will get from the session. Numbers 2 and 3 above speak to the hook, and number 4 speaks to the bait.

Those who know me well or who have read my full biography know that I have a post-secondary teaching background, hence, the reason the title creation strategies are accompanied by several examples of the strategies in action in conference presentation titles that stem from my time in the academic world. The primary focus here is for you to see examples of the strategies so you have a good idea of how to use them when creating your own engaging session titles.

CHART 3: That's Snappy!: Titles That Crackle and Pop

STRATEGIES	EXAMPLES
1. Acronyms: Is there an already established acronym you can use or one you can create?	Now That's What's H-O-T!: Creating Test Questions That Assess Higher Order Thinking Skills
2. Alliteration: Are there words where you can use the repetition of the same consonant sounds or the same kinds of consonant sounds?	Print Your Passion: The Power (and Profitability) of Becoming a Published Author Business Communication 101: Truth, Trust, and Transparency The Must-Have Money-Making Marketing Tool
3. Assonance: Are there words where you can use the repetition of the same vowel sounds or the same kinds of vowel sounds?	Lesson Design for Changing Times
4. Before and after: Can you take two words or two phrases and combine them so they share a word or a portion of a word or phrase?	The Thoroughbred and Butter: Getting Students to Embrace Their Inner Winner! (If I'm not mistaken, this session was offered at a conference that took place on the eve of the Kentucky Derby.)

Continued

CHART 3: That's Snappy!: Titles That Crackle and Pop
(Continued)

STRATEGIES	EXAMPLES
5. Clichés: Can you create a play on a cliché, using a popular expression or common thought to create an original twist to a presentation topic?	Making Horses Thirsty: Increasing Student Motivation to Learn (inspired by "You can take a horse to water, but you can't make it drink.")
6. Company logos/slogans: Can you borrow from the marketing success of established industries?	That's Snappy!: Titles That Crackle and Pop (inspired by Kellogg's Rice Krispies cereal mascots, Snap, Crackle, and Pop)
7. Holidays: Does your session fall on a holiday, and you can tie it into your session title? (Note: It is best to tailor the session title so it still makes sense if the session is offered on another day.)	Tricks Becoming Treats!: How to Use Devices of Distraction as Engines that Educate (could be particularly effective as a play on Halloween but could still be used beyond the holiday)
8. Idioms: Can you use a phrase that means something other than its literal meaning?	It's Time to Spill the Beans!: Discover Why Students Leave and How to Change Their Minds
9. Mathematics: Can you use formulas or the plus sign instead of "and" to join ideas?	$E = mc^2$: Engagement is Mathematically Contextualized Content
10. Metaphors: Is there a comparison you can make between the topic and another object, concept, or idea?	Why Course Redesign is the Bee's Knees (Extremely Good) for Developmental Education

Continued

CHART 3: That's Snappy!: Titles That Crackle and Pop
(Continued)

STRATEGIES	EXAMPLES
11. Opposites: Can you juxtapose antonyms that are standalone words or concepts, or can you create hyphenated words or phrases?	Get the Low-Down on High-Tech: Five BIG Reasons to Add Technology to Your Teaching Open with Power and Close the Deal: Winning Presentation Secrets to Fuel the Move from Prospect to Client Easy Ideas for Hard Conversations: How to Effectively Use Your Voice to Always Say the Right Thing
12. Parallelism: Can you use a parallel structure whereby words have the same or similar beginnings or endings or the same grammatical structure?	The Digital Difference: Engaging Students, Increasing Productivity, and Impacting Success Activities to Accelerate Exceptional Academic Achievement All Sizzle, No Fizzle: How to Deliver Blazing-Hot Presentations
13. Popular culture references: Does a movie, cartoon, sports team, comic strip, or television show lend itself to being part of a session title?	Back to the Future: Examining the Transformation of Educational Technology
14. Puns: Can you make a play on words?	Easy as Pi: 3.14 Ways to Make Math Class Stress-Free for Students Give Students an Author They Can't Refuse: Using Best-Sellers to Influence Students' Desire to Read Turn It App a Notch: Tools for a More Engaging iPad Educational Experience

Continued

CHART 3: That's Snappy!: Titles That Crackle and Pop
(Continued)

STRATEGIES	EXAMPLES
15. Repetition: Can you use the same word or the same phrase multiple times?	The Right Communication At the Right Time With the Right Person For the Right Reason Hear Me, Love Me, Hire Me: Top Secrets from World-Class Speakers on How to Use Presentations to Grow Your Business
16. Rhetorical Questions or the "Voice in Your Head" Statement: Can you identify a rhetorical question that speaks to the attitude surrounding a topic? Is there a challenge or a problem in the back of a person's mind that your session will solve?	Why Isn't Anyone Following Me?!: A Go-Getter's Guide to Leadership and Communication But I Didn't Know I Was Cheating!: Plagiarism—Innocent and Intentional
17. Similes: Is there a positive comparison you can make between the topic and another object, concept, or idea using "like" or "as"?	Like Peas and Carrots: Integrating Reading and Writing with Developmental Students Teach Like a Superhero... No Cape Required
18. Slang: Can you juxtapose slang with your presentation topic?	It's On an' Poppin'!: Surefire Methods That'll Jumpstart Students' Writings about Readings
19. Songs: Can you use a popular or well-known song or lyrics?	Walk That Walk and Talk That Talk: Communication Habits of the Most Confident Leaders (inspired by Rihanna's "Talk That Talk")
20. Start Then Finish: Can you mention a concept in the main title then follow-up in the subtitle with a connection to the concept?	Bringing the Heat: Key Components to Consistently Make Your Trainings Relevant and Red-Hot (This is also contains an example of alliteration.)

CHART 4: Combination Techniques

Alliteration PLUS Assonance:	Attention-Getting Retention Tools and Tips: Practical Ideas for Faculty
Alliteration PLUS Opposites PLUS Repetition:	How to Show Up and Show Out When You Really Want to Just Shut Down
Cliché PLUS Opposites:	Never Let Them See You Sweat: How to Keep Your Cool When Challenging Students Run You Hot
Holiday PLUS Song:	Talk That Talk!: A Guaranteed Approach That'll Make Students Fall In Love with Your Lectures (presented on Valentine's Day and inspired by Rihanna's "Talk That Talk")
Pop Culture PLUS Pun:	Equipping Students with the Write Stuff: Soaring Strategies for Writing Across the Curriculum (inspired by the book and movie *The Right Stuff*)
Pun PLUS Opposites:	Lecture Light Shine: High-Wattage (and Low-Stress) Ideas to Engage Any Student.

---

[1]For a more on power words, see "Your Speech May Be a Victim of Wimpy Words" in chapter 1.

HOW TO PREVENT INFORMATION OVERLOAD

First, to avoid information overload, it requires being selective about what content goes into your presentation. This can be extremely challenging to figure out what to include and what to omit when it seems like everything is important. To address this, think of your content in terms of gold, silver, and bronze nuggets.

The gold nuggets are the three to five items you *must* cover at all costs; these are items that are the bare minimum the audience must receive. Say to yourself "If I have only 15 minutes, then these are the items I must include." The silver nuggets are the five to seven items that stem from the gold nuggets; these are nice to add on but are not absolutely necessary and will not interfere with the audience's understanding of your subject matter. Then, the bronze nuggets are everything else you could discuss if you had all the time in the world.

After that, plan for how you will allow for your audience to stop and think about what the content means.

We speak at a rate of approximately 140 to 180 words per minute, and on average, a listener's comprehension rate is approximately 400 words per minute. While we process information at a faster rate than a person can speak, tests of listening comprehension show the average person listens at only 25 percent efficiency, though.

Speeding up your rate of speech, trying to squeeze in *everything*, only exacerbates matters—that 25 percent in efficiency is definitely on track to take a dip.

The solution to avoid information overload is the 15-5 Take-and-Give Model where you take 10 to 15 minutes to provide information, then give the audience three to five minutes of time to interact, engage, and process. If you talk much longer than 10 to 15 minutes at a time, then the audience will start to lose interest and may check out.[1]

With the 15-5 Take-and-Give Model, the body of a ~60-minute presentation follows this pattern:

1. Speak for 10 to 15 minutes.
2. Provide a question that has the audience engage for three to five minutes.[2]
3. Speak for another 10 to 15 minutes.
4. Then provide another question that has the audience engage for three to five minutes.
5. Speak for 10 to 15 minutes more.
6. Then offer up a third question that serves as the foundation for three to five minutes of audience engagement.

If you plow through your content without incorporating audience engagement, the audience will not have the opportunity to think about what the content means nor will participants connect the new content with prior knowledge. This is akin to pouring down your audience's throat water that flows from a bottomless bottle without giving everyone the opportunity to stop and swallow. It becomes information overload for your audience.

If you have a presentation that is less than 60 minutes in length or if your presentation is part of a collaboration with other speakers, then this time will vary. However, you should always aim to end your speaking portion with audience interaction and processing. When you do so, you demonstrate to everyone that your goal was not to merely talk at them but that you will ensure that they fully understand the content and are in a position to act upon it as a result.

---

[1] This timing is for face-to-face/in-person presentations; however, for timing with webinars, see "10 Best Practices for Creating Maximum Impact in Your Webinars" in chapter 4.

[2] For guidance on how to design great questions to use during these times of engagement, see "Why No One Responds When You Ask 'Are There Any Questions?' And What to Ask Instead" in chapter 3.

3 IDEAS FOR WHAT TO DO WITH ALL THAT CONTENT THAT YOU CANNOT (AND SHOULD NOT) SQUEEZE INTO YOUR PRESENTATION

At this point, you might be thinking "What do I do after I follow the 15-5 Take-and Give Model[1] and I still have a lot of information that I want to share?" Neither you nor your audience is out of luck.

After you organize your presentation, selecting only three to five problems to solve, and you still have additional content, you're in a great position because it keeps the door open to the possibility of future opportunities. Here's what you do with what's left on the cutting room floor.

1. Book another gig.

When you do not give away the entire farm all at once, you have additional content you can use for a follow-up presentation because what's better than one opportunity to get in front of an audience to sell yourself, your company, your worth, your value, your talent, your products, or your services? A second opportunity![2]

2. Build a community.

Either drive them to an online community you've already built or create a social media group that is focused on providing information on the topic on which you presented. Nobody said all information has to be given in a formal presentation. As a matter of fact, people enjoy consuming information from and in a variety of formats. Or if it's your jam, consider a live session on a social media platform, extending a special invitation to your audience, or create a recorded video plus directions in your live session for how to access it.

3. Broaden your reach.

If there are details you did not get to, write a blog post on your website or Medium or LinkedIn article that covers them. And do not mention during the presentation you did not cover XYZ content so you're going to write a blog post about it. Make the audience feel special! Say "As a thank you for your participation and to keep the conversations going, one week from today, I will post a new article about XYZ at www.mywebsite.com so you can extend your learning."

---

[1] For more on the 15-5 Take and Give Model., see "How to Prevent Information Overload" in chapter 3.

[2] Check out *Book More Business: Make Money Speaking* by Lois Creamer for a wealth of information on booking follow-up engagements.

MOVE THEM FROM PASSIVE TO ACTIVE: 3 REALLY EASY AUDIENCE ENGAGEMENT TOOLS

Here are a few of my favorite ways to get the audience involved so it is not a chalk-and-talk or a sit-and-get experience. These techniques require virtually no preparation, and you can easily and expertly insert them into any presentation at any time when you...

1. need everyone to process what you presented;

2. sense a lull; or

3. know you have been talking too much and conclude that it is time for everyone to hear another voice.[1]

One-Minute Conversation

Pose an open-ended question and then have each audience member partner with a colleague and have a conversation; use a timer and let them know when one minute has expired. Ask for volunteers to share the results of their conversations.

Take it to another level: Roam around the room and listen in on conversations. First, this lets the audience know that you are interested in what is being discussed and are not providing a meaningless activity. Second, you are available to conveniently answer any questions that may arise while the conversations continue to flow. Third, you can sprinkle into the remainder of your presentation highlights from the conversations. Finally, circulating around the room helps you keep conversations on topic and on track.

Think it through: You may ask "What if conversations are really robust? Do I stop them at the one-minute mark?" The answer is "No." If you sense the energy in the room is incredibly positive and lively, then let the conversations go another minute or so. However, if time is of the essence, then do stop them. In this case, tell them to turn to a colleague/classmate and commit to continue the conversation later. It helps to seal the deal with a high-five, or a fist bump, or ... well ... you know your style! Pick a "seal the deal" gesture, and roll with it!

One-Minute Paper[2]

Similar to the one-minute conversation, ask an open-ended question and then have the audience members write their responses; use a timer and let them know when one minute has expired. If you see people still writing after one minute has expired, allow for a few more seconds before moving on. The point of the one minute is to make it low-stakes. Ask for volunteers to share what they wrote.

Take it to another level: This activity will also work well if used in the closing to get feedback or for audience members to write down action items. Alternatively, for a class session, this method is useful as a formative assessment to help you determine where to start the next class session. For instance, ask: "What was the most difficult concept in today's class for you to understand?" (And I recommend you already have those concepts listed on a slide or the board as a quick reference point for learners.) Then flip through the responses to quickly glean what needs more attention in the future, either by providing supplemental materials or additional information online or in-person.

Think it through: Because one minute tends to fly by, plan for this activity to run a little longer, and make sure you plan for the activity to take at least five to seven minutes to complete. This way, you provide the directions, give two to three minutes for thinking and writing and to collect the responses. To make the process easier on yourself, provide index cards so all the responses are on the same size paper. This makes going through them more of a breeze. Position yourself at the exit to collect the cards, and thank them for their participation as they depart.

Think-Pair-Share[3]

Pose an open-ended question, have each audience member silently THINK about his or her own answer, and then have each person PAIR with a colleague and have a conversation about their answers for a set amount of time. Once this time expires, ask for volunteers to SHARE the results of or takeaways from their conversations.

Take it to another level: The SHARE can be a SHOUT! When you give directions, inform the audience that you will ask for volunteers to shout out three to five words from their conversations that caught their attention. Write these words on a board or a large PostIt for everyone to see throughout the session. This will serve to remind them of the great ideas their colleagues came up with. (And if you want to get your audience moving, have them stand during the PAIR conversation; just that little bit of movement and change of position changes the energy in a good way![4])

Think it through: Ensure you give the audience members enough time to actually think on their own before insisting they begin conversing. Even suggest they write down their answers first so they all have solid starting points for their conversations. Another option is to have teams of three or four engage in the think-pair-share (as opposed to only two colleagues). This positions a participant who does not like to talk much to gain so much more from listening to others. Finally, one minute is not a set rule. When you feel great energy in the room, feel free to let the minute go a little longer.

---

[1]For more on how to avoid talking too much, see "How to Prevent Information Overload" in chapter 3.

[2]Adapted from Angelo, T. A., & Cross, K. P. (1993). *Classroom assessment techniques*, (2nd ed), pp. 148–153. San Francisco: Jossey-Bass.

[3]Adapted from Lyman, F. Think-pair-share. *MAA-CIE Cooperative News*.

[4]For more ideas on how to get audiences moving, see "How to Ensure You Reach Everyone in the Room" in chapter 3.

HOW TO UNCOMPLICATE A COMPLICATED TOPIC AND EFFORTLESSLY PRESENT ON ANY SUBJECT MATTER

What do you do when you are seriously passionate about an obscure topic on which you are requested to speak? How do you engage the audience? How do you ensure you do not talk over people's heads or that you do not talk down to your audience? How do you avoid fostering a boring experience for yourself (and possibly your audience) by creating overly elementary points? Circumstances such as this can lead to a conundrum—that is for sure.

However, you can still discuss topics that are foreign to others in a way that is engaging for everyone involved. Actually, that is a fundamental purpose of public speaking—to educate others. This simply means you have to find ways to approach or connect your presentation to a topic or concept that is already familiar to your audience. There is a two-step process for accomplishing this.

First, start with the three key questions to answer in your presentations about material that may be new to your audience:[1]

1. What is it?
2. How does one start to understand it?
3. Why is it important, and why should others care?

What happens is you work to relate the unknown or the unfamiliar to what is known or familiar to the audience. Doing so makes it easier for the audience to make connections with your material.

Second, rather than asking "Do you know what I mean?" ask a meaningful question to check for comprehension. When you ask "Do you know what I mean?" if there is indeed a participant who does not know what you mean, it is highly unlikely he or she will say so. This is because he or she may feel embarrassed, as though he or she is the only one who does not know what you mean. Further, the question has the hidden suggestion that the audience *should know* what you mean, so no one really wants to respond.

Exercise extreme caution with asking what you think is a more meaningful question. Presenters will ask what sounds like, on the surface, a meaningful question, but because they have failed to provide the audience with sufficient information beforehand for everyone to arrive at an answer, it can result in silence. As such, it is vital that you provide ample content before you ask a question.[2]

---

[1]Use these questions for the design of every presentation no matter the topic or the audience's level of knowledge or understanding of your topic. Answering what, how, and why is the foundation to creating a top-notch presentation. For realz.

[2]For more on how to provide ample information and how to design effective questions, see "How to Prevent Information Overload" and "Why No One Responds When You Ask 'Are There Any Questions?' and What to Ask Instead," respectively, in chapter 3.

REFLECT, REVIEW, AND RESPOND: DO YOU KNOW HOW TO GIVE EVERYONE A REASON TO LISTEN TO YOU?

1. What question do presentations often fail to answer? Why is it critical for a presenter to ensure every presentation answers this question?

2. How do you grab your audience's attention no matter your topic?

3. How effective is the start of your presentations? What will you do differently going forward?

4. Why do jokes flop when presenters use them to start a presentation? Should you or should you not crack jokes anywhere in your presentations? Explain.

5. How do you prevent yourself from rambling or from getting too far off-topic when you present?

6. How do you expertly engage the audience without a lot of bells, whistles, games, and antics?

7. Why do you get no response when you ask "Are there any questions?" What should you ask your audience instead?

8. How do you get your audience excited before your presentation even starts?

9. How much is too much information, and what do you do to ensure you do not overload your audience with too much information?

10. What are three simple ways to move your audience from been passive listeners to active participants?

11. What is the simplest approach to present information that may be complicated for your audience?

Chapter 4

DELIVER ABSOLUTELY FLAWLESS PRESENTATIONS

Chapter 4

DELIVER ABSOLUTELY FLAWLESS PRESENTATIONS

If you think making a presentation is just talking, then we have a lot of work to do.

When you see a perfectly polished presenter who moves effortlessly, what you see on public display is countless hours of work that's been performed in private.

They have a flawless methodology for making flawless presentations. And to get to the point where you consistently make flawless presentations, it takes a methodology, and it takes work. A lot of work. There is no magic bullet. It is not easy and does not happen overnight. It takes patience and a willingness to repeatedly critique yourself and make improvements where you constantly ask yourself "What can I do differently next time that will lead to a better performance than the last?"

When you have a methodology for designing your presentations as opposed to just showing up and talking, you get closer to becoming a more confident, more powerful, and more dynamic speaker. You will not leave the stage kicking yourself because you forgot to iterate a point or because you did not masterfully address a challenging audience member. You will not *hope* you nailed your presentation. You will *know* you drove home every point, that you handled questions like a pro, and that you *unequivocally* nailed it. Now that, my friend, is a good feeling.

Going forward, give the presentation you would want to see and experience if you were in the audience. Plain and simple.

In this chapter, you will know how to ...

- organize your presentation for maximum impact and so you immediately grab everyone's attention
- have purposeful movements to support your message
- employ nonverbal communication tactics to show confidence, authority, control, and honesty

- expertly conclude your presentation so everyone knows that your presentation was time well spent
- open and close sales presentations without feel overly sales-y or incredibly uncomfortable
- make smart decisions about delivering webinars

THE ONLY PRESENTATION PLAN YOU WILL EVER NEED PART 1: BEHIND THE SCENES

Much of a presentation's success lies with how well the presenter prepares and how well he or she avoids leaving any facet of an event, workshop, webinar, meeting, training, or presentation to chance. There are those who call it controlling, but I like to think of it as controlling the power of your message before anyone else takes control of it. Period.

REAL TALK PRINCIPLE

Take control of your message before anyone else takes control of it.

Prior to show time, put in place as many components as possible so when you are ready to perform, you know you have left little to chance, and just like that—you have an instant confidence boost. These nine are a must:

1. Ask for everything you need.

You know what you need for your presentation to be a success. Instead of worrying about whether the event contact or the venue will come through, clarify precisely what you need.

Create your own list, and communicate that list of requests beforehand to confirm the items will be made available for your presentation. Sure, there are items on which you may get a "no," and that is fine. You do not know what the event contact will provide if you do not ask.[1]

2. Consider when and where you are presenting.

Familiarity leads to comfort, which leads to confidence. Travel the route well before the presentation and visit the room in which you will present at least two hours before your meeting so when it is time to go to the presentation, you know where you are going and are in familiar surroundings.

- How long does it take to get the presentation venue?

- Where is the most ideal or permissible location to park? Is a cost involved? Will you need a decal?

- Confirm with your contact you will be able to you gain access to the room at least two hours before the presentation starts. Who will be the one to provide you access?

- If applicable, will WiFi and Internet access be available?

- What is your Plan B if you need Internet access? (Will you provide your own device that enables remote access? Will you include in your presentation screenshots of the web-pages you had planned to visit?)

- Who should you contact to help with setup and audio/visual needs? Indicate you will need this person to be available at least one hour before your presentation start time to test all A/V and at the start of the presentation to ensure everything is still working properly. Get this person's contact information in the event you need to reach out if there is a problem with A/V during the course of your presentation.

3. What handouts/leave-behinds, if any, will you provide?

Methodically think through this because handouts and leave-behinds can contribute to any small glitch that interferes with the powerful flow you have going with your presentation. Again, you want every detail—or as many details as possible—carefully orchestrated. This concept might be frightening at first, but once you create for yourself a plan of approach, you will have it as your foundation for every presentation.

For those handouts and leave-behinds (brochures, URLs, instructions, et cetera) that are not critical to the audience's ability to follow along with your presentation, distribute them at the end of the session. For handouts that participants will need during the presentation, distribute them after you have welcomed everyone, thanked the audience for coming, announced what everyone will know or be able to do by the end of the session, given the agenda items, and introduced yourself—and in that order.[2] Alternatively, you can provide the handouts before the start of the session, placing them face down at participants' seats. And a green option of digital handouts and/or supplements is even better.

Ensure your handout or leave-behind is designed to not take away from your in-person message; avoid putting so much on the handout until the audience can simply read/review it and tune out on your verbal presentation. Consider providing guided notes where your key points are listed, but there are blanks participants have to fill in as they listen; this helps with keeping them focused and reiterating your content.

- What handout and/or leave-behind will you provide?

- When is the most ideal time to distribute the handout, during the presentation or at the end? (Distribute at the beginning if it contains content the audience will need to access during your presentation. Distribute afterwards if it serves as a reference and is not critical to the audience understanding your presentation.)

- Should you provide a QR code or some other means of linking to the handout, email the handout, or have it as a leave-behind for audience members after the session?

4. Clarify if food will be a part of the presentation.

This point is particularly relevant to individuals who make sales presentations. Unless instructed otherwise, refreshments are usually a plus in a sales presentation. Now, I am a bit on the fence regarding providing food at presentations, but many, especially professionals involved in selling academic products and services, tend to find doing so is greatly appreciated by audience members. (And as a former faculty member myself who was never one to turn down a free lunch, I get it!). To avoid having to focus on this detail at all and to place all the emphasis on the presentation, it is advisable to have a presentation during a time when food is not necessarily expected such as 9:00 a.m., 10:00 a.m., 2:00 p.m., or 3:00 p.m. with a preference on the morning hours to avoid having an audience plagued by afternoon fatigue or a post-lunch slump. Take care of these details in advance.

- Are you bringing snacks?

- Are you having a meal catered by a private company?

- Are you having a meal catered through the client to whom you are presenting?

- Will another contact take care of snacks and/or a meal? If so, then who?

- At what point will audience members be invited to partake of the snacks or the meal, and how much time will you allot for everyone to serve him or herself? Time this so it does not detract from you and your message. Consider announcing food will be available 15 to 20 minutes before the start of the presentation and that the presentation will start promptly at the appointed time.

5. Get a POWER OUTFIT!

Make sure you feel good and look good, that you are ready to take control! A stylist or an image consultant is of great benefit here, or if you have a trusted fashion-conscious friend with the right eye for styles flattering to you and your personality, then reach out for guidance with making ideal professional attire choices. Plus, you can always enlist the help of a department store sales associate to find the perfect look and fit for you. Dark colors such as navy, charcoal, chocolate, and black are best for a professional look; keep accessories and light colors or accent colors to a minimum. In short, know what works for your body type, avoid trendy styles, and lean toward more classic looks.

- What colors most make you feel confident and look confident to others?

- What one to three outfits do you already have that project you in the best and most professional light possible? (In recent years, I have adopted a practice of wearing all black in my in-person presentations; it's easy, it stands up to stains, and it allows the audience to focus on my words more than my outfit. For webinars, I tend to wear other colors that are better suited for being on camera.[3])

6. Be aware of slide design.

Keep words on your slides to a minimum. Make your images larger, and reduce the amount of text you have on your slides to make for a more engaging deck. For example, instead of using a bulleted list of information on a slide, give each item of information its own slide. Resize and position a high-quality image so it covers the entire slide, and include a text box containing the one bullet of information, centered over the image. Or better yet, have nothing but an image on a slide with no text at all. My favorite sites for locating high-resolution, royalty-free images are pexels.com, pixabay.com, and unsplash.com. When you search for images on a stock photography site (e.g., an image of a boat), try different synonyms of the word (e.g., ship), specific types or categories of the word (e.g., yacht, steamboat, canoe, et cetera), or related words (e.g., fishing, sailing, cruise, et cetera).

Use a thesaurus or keyword lists on the actual image pages to identify other keywords to use in your image search.

Make font selections and choose font sizes that are easy for the audience to read. Avoid the use of fancy, flowery fonts; they are difficult for the audience to see. Fonts such as Arial, Avenir, Helvetica, Raleway, Tahoma, and Times New Roman work well. And always make sure your font is large enough—at least 28 point for bulleted content and at least 32 point for headers—so your audience can actually see the text no matter the font you use. If you ever wonder whether your audience can see a slide, print it out on 8.5" × 11" paper, place it on the floor, and read it from a standing position. if you can make it out, then your slide is good to go!

If you have a complicated slide, highlight only the portion of the slide that has relevance for your listeners. You may also show the entire slide, then have a second slide where you have zoomed in on the pertinent information that you want to get your audience's attention, fully and clearly depicting a portion of the previous (complicated) slide.

Additionally, choose the appropriate background color and font color for your slides to ensure the audience can easily see and read the information. If you have an audience size of 50 or fewer audience members, then design your slides with a light or white background along with text that is black or dark in color. If your audience size is larger than 50, then design your slides with a dark or black background along with text that is a light in color.

Consistently aim to use those fonts and to locate and use those images that support your message, that grab the audience's attention, that make the audience think, and that provide for a polished and professional look. Standard clipart is not sufficient. Low-resolution images—you know, the ones that look fuzzy, especially when you try to resize them—make presentations look amateurish. Similarly, placing multiple small images on a slide with no strategy for doing so has the same effect. Always always always use high-quality, high-resolution graphics so your images are not pixilated, unattractive, and/or hard to discern. In short, ensure your information is not derailed by a poorly designed slide deck.

Have a consistent theme throughout your presentation; there should not be a multitude of templates; it looks tacky and unprofessional. That's fine if you pull slides from a variety of presentations to put together a new session. Do the work in choosing a color scheme and a font family that you apply to the entire presentation so it doesn't look like a bunch of different presentations have been amateurly slapped together to create a new one.

Finally, avoid including slides that serve no purpose. Ask yourself, for each slide, what you want the audience to think, how you want it to feel, or what you want it to do. If a slide does not have an audience thinking, feeling, or acting, then it does not belong in your deck. Similarly, avoid including a slide and simultaneously telling your audience "I'm just going to speed through this," "I know you cannot read this," or "I know this is hard to see." If a slide is worthy of only a "speed-through" or if the audience cannot read or clearly see a slide's contents, then it serves no purpose. Revise, redesign, or remove it.

A great resource on slide design is Nancy Duarte's *Slide:ology: The Art and Science of Creating Great Presentations.* Add it to your library.

7. Identify two or three audience engagement tools you will use at any given moment.

Three of my favorite audience engagement tools are think-pair-share, one-minute conversation, and a one-minute paper. They require few to no materials and involve simple directions for the audience.[4]

Because the power of the tool lies in the question asked and not so much in the tool itself, feel free to use the exact same engagement tool multiple times throughout the same presentation Ask good questions, questions that have the audience think, questions that will get people thinking of your topic in a positive light, questions that are open-ended and call for more than a one-word answer are the key to this tool working and working well time and time again.

- What is at least one engagement tool you will use in your presentation?
- What questions will you ask?
- At what point(s) will you use the tool(s)?

8. Consider any and everything on which prospective participants might push back.

Make sure you have all the issues out in the open beforehand. Know the participants' needs, and tailor the presentation to align with them. If you have the answers to issues, address them as early as possible in the presentation to avoid having tension bubbling underneath the surface.[5]

- What are their concerns already on the table?

- What solution(s) should you present?

- How do you answer this question/address this concern?

- Which will require research and need to be answered later or via email?

- How will you communicate you will get back with an answer to any concerns not addressed in the presentation?

9. Know who will attend the presentation.

Google is your friend. If you present to a small team or committee, know a few details about everyone in the room. It is not necessary that you openly use this information during the presentation; use it to gain a good idea of your audience and more information about participants than you will get during the course of any introductions. In the event the opportunity presents itself to engage in a casual conversation, then incorporating into the conversation details from your desktop research is appropriate, but avoid prefacing it with "I checked out your LinkedIn profile, and I saw that you once lived in … ." It sounds trite, and it makes you appear slightly like a stalker; simply state, "So you once lived in … ." If the person happens to ask from whence you got the information, then you oblige him or her by revealing your source.[6]

- What is the average age of your audience?

- What is the range of years of experience?

- What points about the participants can you glean that are relative to your topic?

---

[1]For comprehensive lists of what to request, see "The Only Presentation Plan You Will Ever Need Part 3: Your Quick and Clean Checklist" in chapter 4.

[2]For more on a methodology for starting your presentation, see "The Only Presentation Plan You Will Ever Need Part 2: The Actual Presentation" in chapter 4.

[3]For more on colors that are better suited for wearing in a webinar environment, see "Virtually Everything Matters in a Virtual Presentation" in chapter 4.

[4]For more on audience engagement and engagement tools, see "Audience Engagement Done Right," "Why No One Responds When You Ask 'Are There Any Questions?' and What to Ask Instead," as well as "Move Them From Passive to Active: 3 Really Easy Audience Engagement Tools" in chapter 3.

[5]For more on how to address difficult audience members, see "Never Again Get Derailed by a Difficult Audience Member" in chapter 5.

[6]For more on analyzing the audience, see "How Well Do You Really Know Your Audience?" in chapter 2.

THE ONLY PRESENTATION PLAN YOU WILL EVER NEED PART 2: THE ACTUAL PRESENTATION

Once you have planned the behind-the-scenes portion of your presentation, it is time to dive into the actual presentation. Here is the three-part format for writing your script and organizing your presentation. This enables you to immediately grab everyone's attention, clarify to the audience why everyone should listen to you, and create engagement the right way. Again, this takes time and conscious thought.

REAL TALK PRINCIPLE

Making presentations that sizzle is not getting up, winging it.

Include these three parts—each of which has its own set of steps—in your presentation preparation and design, and you will provide a flawless presentation …

- power opening
- power body
- power closing

But before you actually start your presentation, take advantage of some really grand opportunities to connect with your audience.

One way is to stand at the entrance and welcome everyone to your session with a handshake or just a "thank you for coming" message as each person enters the room. What's cool about this is the obvious—you're greeting people and showing appreciation for their presence—but also when you start your presentation, it does not feel like you are staring out into a sea of strangers. Because you have met several of those assembled, as you scan the audience, there are familiar faces that can provide some level of comfort.

A second way to create a connection with your audience before the official start to your presentation is to solve problems right away. This is an absolute FAVORITE technique of mine. AS a matter of fact, it's imperative that I arrive to my room several minutes before the official start time to ensure I have my technology set up so I can make sure I have tons of time before the session starts to engage early arrivers by answering their questions. Here's what I mean: In those instances where you have several participants who arrive to the session early and you are already set and ready to present, engage the audience by asking questions such as "What is a problem you want solved relative to X?" or "What have you always wanted to know about X?" with "X" being your presentation topic. Give answers in real-time, and participants absolutely love it! They do! I recall a participant at a conference in New York City who told me, at the end of my presentation, that because of my pre-session engagement where I responded to presentation skills challenges posed by audience members right there on the spot, she felt even more compelled to remain for the entire presentation. My taking questions early on caused her to immediately see me as someone who was credible and someone who was in command of the presentation topic. She (and everyone else present) received value before the presentation even started.

Power Opening

- start on time

- welcome and express gratitude

- connect, toggle, and provide benefits (objectives)

- provide the agenda

- give your power intro

- clarify how you will handle questions

1. Start on Time

When you begin and end a presentation as scheduled, you show respect for the audience's time. When you fail to do either or both, you send the message that "My presentation and my time are more important than your time." Plain and simple.

Your audience members who have shown respect by arriving early or on time are due the same respect. You may wonder what to do when factors arise that delay your presentation. For instance, you may have a glitch with the technology or a person in a key position has yet to arrive.

If that or any other instance is the case, then let the audience know at the official start time and proceed to engage everyone in a meaningful exercise. A quick statement to this effect works: "Thank you for coming today. We are fixing a technical glitch." Or "Thank you for coming today. We do not want to begin without your division chairperson. We will get started shortly. In the meantime, please write down what you want to get out of today's session, then discuss it with the colleague sitting next to you."

2. Welcome and Express Gratitude

This is akin to opening the front door to your home and letting guests know you are pleased to have them there with you. Stand front and center throughout the entire power opening and offer a simple "Welcome to the session" or "Thank you for coming." When you show gratitude, you create a positive atmosphere; it conveys that all is well and that you are in control. In short, it demonstrates for both you and your audience that you have confidence from the start.

3. Connect, Toggle, and Provide Benefits (Objectives)

Inform everyone as to why they should listen to you, toggling between the challenges they will continue to face if they do not have the information you provide as well as the benefits they will experience with the information you provide. To do this, you must answer three specific questions beforehand to get at the heart of what everyone needs: What are the audience's challenges? With what does the audience need help? What does the audience want to improve? Then, in the body of your presentation, solve only three to five problems, and do so as succinctly as possible. Give only what they must know, not every single angle there is to know about the topics. Remember you are not making experts out of your listeners. Rather, you have two options: Tell them a few items and know they got it or tell them everything and walk away, wondering if any of it stuck. At this point, you identify what the audience will know or be able to do by the end of the presentation.[1]

4. Provide the Agenda

Provide and explain agenda items, showing how you will achieve the aforementioned, e.g., "We will accomplish this by examining X, reviewing Y, discussing Z...."[2]

5. Give Your Power Intro

Give your name and a one- to two-sentence statement explaining how what you do helps members be better at what they do, e.g. "My name is Bridgett McGowen, and what I do is I help professionals be the most dynamic, engaging, incredible communicators ever!" (Avoid giving a job title because titles mean nothing, especially to those outside of your organization...well...possibly to those inside your organization, too!) Notice I recommend the presenter wait until AFTER letting the audience know how its time will be spent before you provide your name. The audience wants to know how its time will be spent. They want to know what it is you do that will help everyone seated before you live better, work better, and perform better. Many will argue that providing the audience with the speaker's biography is key to establishing one's credibly. However, credibility is established only when you demonstrate the presentation's utility and when you immediately provide value.[3]

6. Clarify How You Will Handle Questions

Explain how you will handle questions Will you take them throughout the presentation, at certain points, or only at the end?[4]

Power Body

- inform the audience

- engage the audience

- capitalize on nonverbal communication

- transition

7. Inform the Audience

Television has conditioned audiences to expect fast-paced, attention-grabbing methods of information delivery. If you want to engage as many people as possible and if you want people to retain what you state, then you must create opportunities that aim to meet the television-conditioned learning needs and that take into account the shorter attention spans of your audiences. More specifically, you should break up your information delivery into shorter segments while increasing audience involvement. Provide no more than 10 to 15 minutes of information before you change the pace and give participants time to engage and think about what you provided. This timing is not a firm rule, but if you talk much longer than this, then the audience will start to lose interest and check out.[5]

8. Engage the Audience

Allow for three to five minutes of audience interaction and processing. Have the audience use the information you presented to think of what everyone will do differently with this new knowledge. (Again, if you have a shorter presentation, then this time will vary.) Remember the power of engagement lies in the power of the questions you ask. When you draw in the audience with great questions, this helps everyone remember what you presented. It demonstrates the importance of the information because you are devoting time to having everyone process what you presented. You are showing the audience that you do not want to talk at them but that you want to ensure they fully understand your message. This will position them to act on what you said.

To do this, do not ask "Are there any questions?" or "Does that make sense?" You will get crickets. Audience engagement done right means you ask great questions. Decide if you will have them talk, write, listen, or move, then if you want to excite, change behavior, apply information, or think big picture.[6]

Repeat numbers 7 and 8, volleying back and forth until you complete your presentation.

9. Capitalize on Non-Verbal Language

First, know what your body language will express at every point of your presentation. Start front and center with your opening. Then, punctuate your points by standing in and/or looking to different parts of the room as you cover each one. If you have three points to cover, then move to the left side of the room to discuss the first point, the middle of the room to discuss the second point, and the right side of the room to discuss the third point. If you have a short presentation, then front and center is ideal; you have the option to move a short distance to the left and the right to make eye contact with everyone. Doing so makes you look natural as you speak as opposed to looking like a statue stuck in one place. However, if your presentation is a short one, then moving too much and too far is distracting.

Additionally, keep the following points in mind as you incorporate body language into your presentation:[7]

a. When you stand with your feet about a shoulder width apart, it signals that you feel in control.

b. When people are nervous, their hands often flit about and fidget. When they are confident, they are still. To help keep your body language under control, imagine a box in front of your chest and belly and contain your hand movements within it.

c. Another indicator of confidence and control is to gesture as if you are holding a basketball between your hands. It looks as if you have the facts at your fingertips.

d. To show you are relaxed, clasp both hands together in a relaxed pyramid. Many business executives employ this gesture.

e. To indicate openness and honesty, gesture with the palms of your hands up. It shows we are all in this together.

f.   If you want to show strength, authority and assertiveness, then use the opposite movement with the palms of your hands facing downward.

Use your voice and the power of the pause to make certain that you are in control of words and your presentation.[8] This does not mean you need to speak loudly. It means you speak with energy, authority, and passion.

10. Transition

Audience questions will naturally occur at this point. If you opt to take questions throughout your presentation, then now is the time to address them.[4] Afterwards, provide the appropriate transition to the next topic by conducting the following:

a.   **Review:** Let everyone know the topic you just covered.

b.   **Preview:** Give a preview of the topic you are about to move on to.

c.   **Give the Big View:** If it's not abundantly obvious, tell the audience how the previewed agenda items fit with the entire presentation and how it advances the presentation's overall objective.

Failure to provide a review, preview, and big view can result in confused and frustrated audiences and can lead to difficult audience members engaging in sidebar conversations and/or asking challenging questions. Although, as the presenter, it may sound like you're going overboard by giving a preview, review, and big view, but keep in mind you've heard these ideas over and over again while your audience is hearing them for the first time.

To illustrate this, I will use a sample script from a presentation about presentation skills. Before I transition from one agenda item to the next, I would say...

a. "We just covered how to establish your credibility and the fact it does not lie in a moderator reading your bio or an introduction." (REVIEW)

b. "Next, we will cover how to get your audiences to lean in and listen as well as the number 1 reason adults will listen to you." (PREVIEW)

c. "Both of these practices are integral to creating presentations that sizzle because once you establish yourself as a credible professional and once you know what to say in your opening words to get everyone's attention, you set-up yourself to deliver an engaging presentation." (BIG VIEW)

Again, giving the big view is optional but highly recommended. It all depends on how complicated your content is as to whether you should give the big view; however, you will never go wrong if you do all three.

They keep your audience on track, reduce confusion, keep sidebar conversations to a minimum, and position difficult audience members to remain at bay. Without giving those three views, your audiences members are left to figure out how all the content fits together, and with so many mental distractions vying for your listeners' attention, the easier you can make it for them to connect the dots, the better.

Power Closing

- recap

- Q&A and CTA

- express gratitude

- end on time

11. Recap

Succinctly review what big ideas you provided so you know for sure everyone heard the most important takeaways. The recap is as simple as returning to the promise you made in your introduction with you saying "Today, I promised you would know [list objectives]."

12. Q&A and CTA

If you did not address questions throughout the presentation, then address them now. Plus, provide a call to action (CTA) because once you get to the end of your presentation, you do not want your listeners to say "Okay. That was nice. What was the point?" Sample calls to action are: "email me with X," "talk to me afterwards about Y," "schedule a time to discuss Z with me," or "follow me on ABC social media outlet." The "talk to me afterwards" option works best if there is a smaller group and if time permits. If you do tell them to email you, make sure to clarify the purpose of the email. Is it to get more information on what you discussed? Is it to create a strategy for their next moves based on what you stated? Make sure the audience members know why they are emailing you or scheduling a time for a discussion. Provide your contact information more than once and in more than one format. Give the information verbally and in writing (though in writing is preferred). Avoid simply saying "email me" without telling people how they may do so. (Failing to provide contact information is such a pet peeve of mine. It seems so obvious that if you want a person to reach you, you will tell one *how* to reach you! I recall driving and listening to a local radio station when the disc jockey announced he was giving away tickets to an upcoming taco festival—I love good Mexican food! But aside from the fact I love delicious south of the border fare, he was *really* hyping up this event! He said all you had to do was be the tenth caller, and voilà, the tickets were yours. I had my phone in hand—I know. I know; but at least I wasn't texting and driving! I had my phone ready with the keypad in view, poised with my right thumb, ready to go, to start dialing when I heard … a car insurance commercial! Can you *believe* that?! I was beside myself! "You're not going to tell me how to call in?! *Seriously?!* I don't have your number saved in my contacts, dude!" You already know I threw down the phone and changed the station! Tangent. I know. But you get my point. If you want folks to reach out to you, then give them the information they will need in order to actually reach out!)

13. Express Gratitude
Thank the audience with your spoken words, not with a slide. Leave a positive final impression by ending on an energetic note.

Instead of putting the words "thank you" on a concluding slide, put your contact information on it.

14. End on Time

Avoid using phrases such as "If I had more time, I would…" or "For those of you who are available to remain a few minutes after the presentation, I will tell you…." This type of rhetoric suggests that it is the organizer's or the audience's fault that you do not have more time, and that one of those parties was careless in scheduling "such a short amount of time" for you. Additionally, it is unfair to penalize people—positioning them to miss out on additional content—for operating in accordance with the advertised start and end times of the presentation.

Audience participation can become so robust that you may find you need to jettison material. Identify during your practice time what information can be omitted. This way, you are prepared to omit certain material if you fall victim to a time crunch. Decide what information you can leave out that will not interfere with the audience understanding your message as a result of having heard your presentation. If you must do this, simply omit the information without any mention to the audience, and keep it moving. You are the only one who will know what you did not cover. Better yet, you may even have a piece of material that now positions you to schedule a follow-up performance![5]

---

[1] Return to "The One and Only Way to Ever Start Your Presentation" in chapter 3 to see exactly how this opening is done.

[2]For more on providing the agenda, see "How to Grab Your Audience's Attention No Matter Your Topic" in chapter 3.

[3]For more on how to create your power intro, see chapters 2 and 3.

[4]For more on the advantages and disadvantages of the different ways to handle how and when you take questions, see "Stop Taking Questions at the End of Your Presentation" in chapter 5.

[5]For more on timing your talk, see "The Problem with Asking 'How Am I Looking On Time?' and How to Fix It" in chapter 5.

[6]For more on audience engagement, see chapter 3.

[7]For more on body language, see "The Body Language That's Required to Own the Room" in chapter 2.

[8]For more on using pauses, see "The Power of the Pause: 9 Types of Pauses You Need to Add to Your Presentations" in chapter 3.

THE ONLY PRESENTATION PLAN YOU WILL EVER NEED PART 3: YOUR QUICK AND CLEAN CHECKLIST

When I was a faculty development consultant, I traveled virtually every week, making presentations at one college, university, or another to teams of faculty on best practices for the twenty-first century post-secondary classroom. I recall one of the first times I forgot an item on one of those trips; I had left my company credit card at home and had to cover all purchases with my own dime then get reimbursed by my employer. However, the item I forgot is not the focus here. What I did as a result of forgetting the item is more important. I immediately created a checklist for those trips.

Here you go.

You're welcome.

Session Details

- Presentation title
- Presentation description and objectives
- Date, start time, and end time
- Venue name and address
- Room name/number
- Special directions
- Audience demographics

- Audience size
- Organizer's contact information

One Week Before Presentation

- Practice your presentation at least three times all the way through, full-out, as if your audience is right there with you.[1]
- Email the event contact with this script and with "Check-In" as the subject line:

I will arrive at VENUE NAME, located at VENUE STREET ADDRESS, CITY AND STATE, by LOCAL TIME on MONTH, DAY, AND YEAR OF PRESENTATION. I am preparing for up to NUMBER participants for my presentation taking place from START TIME until END TIME.

Thank you for providing LIST EQUIPMENT AND/OR SUP-PLIES THE ORGANIZER PROMISED TO SUPPLY. I will have EQUIPMENT AND/OR SUPPLIES YOU PROMISED TO SUPPLY with me.

If you have questions or if any of this is incorrect, then please let me know by MONTH, DAY, AND YEAR THAT IS THREE BUSINESS DAYS OUT FROM THE DATE OF THE EMAIL MESSAGE.

Looking forward to it!

Thanks so much, ORGANIZER'S NAME!

One Day Before Travel

- Pack
  - Watch or other timepiece such as a smartphone
  - Toothbrush, toothpaste, and deodorant (Bear in mind not every hotel offers that handy-dandy convenience of providing guests with toiletries; and even if you stay in one that does, it is not likely it will have your favorite antiperspirant in powder fresh or ocean breeze scent!)
  - Hairbrush and comb
  - Spare outfit to include a spare pair of shoes
  - Water bottle
  - Snacks: fruit, energy bar, nuts, et cetera
  - Throat lozenges and breath mints
  - Aspirin/emergency medication
  - Bandages and a small tube of antibiotic ointment
- Confirm arrival and departure times with the public transportation outlets you will use for both air and ground travel as applicable.
- Practice your presentation at least once all the way through, full-out; if time does not permit, then, at a minimum, practice the first 10 minutes and the last 10 minutes at least three times full-out.[1]
- Get a good night's sleep.
- Avoid consumption of …

- ○ Alcohol: For the obvious reasons and because it dries the vocal cords.

- ○ Dairy (milk, ice cream, yogurt, cheese) and orange juice: They tend to cause a build-up of mucous in your throat, necessitating repeated (and distracting) clearing of the throat.

- ○ New foods: If your system is not accustomed to it, then it could signal trouble ahead.

- ○ Caffeinated drinks (soda and coffee): These beverages act as diuretics, and you do not want to have to interrupt your presentation to visit the facilities.

- ○ Beans and certain vegetables such as cabbages, broccoli, onions, leeks, radishes, and potatoes: Gas and bloating can follow meals that contain these foods.

- Consume...
  - ○ Water
  - ○ Salads
  - ○ Vegetables
  - ○ Fruits

- Venue map, especially if visiting a location that has multiple buildings

- Boarding passes/train tickets

- Passport/travel ID

- Local currency/cash/credit card

- Route among airport, hotel, and/or venue

- Ground transportation reservations/access to and set-up of ride share app

Venue (Day of Arrival or Day of Presentation)

- Visit the venue or review the room floor plan at least two hours before the start of your presentation; visiting the day before is even better.
- Confirm availability and operation of equipment.
- Check venue's WiFi quality, if required for your presentation, and ask for back-up connection and login credentials.

Electronics and Supplies Presentation (Review before you travel and upon arrival to the venue)

- Laptop or desktop/CPU; tablet; or smartphone and chargers
- Back-up devices and battery packs
- Projector connection adapter
- Travel speakers
- Microphone (A lavalier or lapel mic is the preference.[2])
- Presentation remote/clicker/presenter, charger, and batteries
- Extension cord
- Timer (or use the timer on your smartphone)
- Notepad, pens, and pencils (arrange for the venue or contact person to supply them to keep you from weighing you down as you travel)

- Video camera or smart phone
- Tripod for phone or camera stand
- Wireless router/mobile Wi-Fi hotspot
- Brochures and business cards

Presentation (Review before you travel and upon arrival to the venue)

- Printed introduction for host to read (Control how you are introduced, but still introduce yourself the way you want to be introduced in your presentation or provide your own introduction.[3])
- Physical copy of slides and speaking notes
- Presentation backup (Email it to yourself, or save it to a USB flash drive.)
- Props or samples
- Markers, flip chart, and whiteboard
- Handouts
- Evaluation forms (Instead of a full form, consider using index cards, and have participants write on one side of the index card what worked well for them in the presentation and on the flip side, what they would still like to know relative to the presentation topic or suggestions for how to improve the presentation. Use the latter—suggestions for improvement—if you have thick skin and/or are ready for that kind of feedback. To be green, consider an electronic eval.)

Presentation Day

- Engage in moderate exercise in the morning but only if you already have an established exercise routine; if you do not already exercise on a regular basis, then do not try out this new little adventure in fitness on the day of a presentation!

- Practice your presentation one last time.

- Arrive early, at least 45 minutes before.

- Meet the organizers, hosts, and technicians.

- Test your equipment, and conduct a sound check.

- Prepare speaking area (flip charts, et cetera).

- Ensure proper seating/no blocked views.

- Adjust lights, window treatments, and temperature.

- Locate the restrooms.

- Have a bottle of water with a cap, not a glass or other open container, in your presentation area. The water should be at room temperature because if it is too hot or too cold, then it has negative effects on the vocal chords. Drink only when the audience is engaged in discussion, not in the middle of your presentation, especially if you are making an important point. Be as inconspicuous as possible.

Day After

- Review feedback from evaluation forms or index cards; reflect, and make notes of ideas for improvement. (I tend to wait *far* more than a day or two because I do not want one negative comment in a sea of glowing evals to derail my good feelings I have from the result of delivering what I believe is a sizzling hot presentation.)

- Send invoice, if applicable, and a "thank you" to the organizer, and offer results-based feedback from the session.

- Call the organizer within 48 hours to discuss next steps (webinar, blog series, video conference Q&A, et cetera) to further learning and to ensure the audience actually puts in place the recommendations you made in your presentation.

- Add to your email list or address book any participants' contact information you received.

- Email participants with follow-up materials or digital assets, if applicable.

- Connect with new contacts on social media.

---

[1]For details on how to practice full-out, see "Why You Get Nervous Before a Presentation and the Expert Practice Strategy Guaranteed to Change That" in chapter 1.

[2]For more on microphones, see "Use a Mic. End of Story." in chapter 5.

[3]Read more in "The Way You Have Been Introducing Yourself to Your Audience is All Wrong" and "No Impressive Bio or Background? No Problem!" in chapter 2.

OPEN WITH POWER AND CLOSE THE DEAL: CONSIDERATIONS FOR HOW TO EFFECTIVELY START AND CONDUCT A SALES PRESENTATION

There are five words every professional in wants to hear after making a sales presentation. "Say no more. I'm sold!"

But what can you do to move leads closer to uttering those five words after your sales presentations?

Because you know when you don't get them to buy, you've missed opportunities to lock in new business.

In short, you leave money on the table.

However, when you have a strategy and know how to open with power and, more importantly, close the business, not only do you win but so does your prospect.

But most sales presentations fail because prospects are usually …

- skeptical about a new product's performance/service's results
- unable to see the need for the product or service
- satisfied with the existing product/service
- quick to see what they already have as the status quo with no need to make any changes

And when you show up with your sales presentation, it's often because you and/or the company you represent is...

- convinced its product or service works
- incredibly likely to see a need for the product/service
- dissatisfied with the existing substitute
- set on viewing its product/service as the benchmark

It's not enough for a new product or service to simply be better. Unless the gains far outweigh the losses, prospect will not adopt it.

The good news is you can influence how prospects perceive these gains and losses, and one of the best ways to prove value is to have a powerful opening to your presentations that contrasts life before and after your product/service.

Some of the typical ways of opening presentations include providing a run-down of your experience, education, or background or listing company history or current projects, which typically bores audiences.

Alternately, you can dive right in with your product or service; however, that can be equally problematic because you have not painted a picture of the stakes.

Here is how you start your presentation with power:

- Paint a picture of the prospect's current world; this requires learning as much about the lead as possible beforehand.

- Paint an image of what their world will be like with your product or service; they need to immediately see you fitting into their world.

- Create the bridge for how to get there; demonstrate how your product or service makes it all possible.

Here's a sample script that follows these steps:

> Right now, your team/clients/customers are experiencing ... and this is causing [undesirable results/impact].

> With [your company's product/service], your team/clients/customers will have [desirable results/impact].

> And that's possible because [your company's service/product] does offers [list benefits, not features].

When you start this way, you build rapport and lead with solutions. Those are two of the five ingredients necessary for a successful sales presentation.

Next, present your product or service, giving three to five benefits of purchasing or adopting either. Avoid telling them everything there is to know as well as discussing features; you do not want to talk so much until you overwhelm or bore them, plus people buy benefits, not features. For instance, as opposed to a car salesperson telling you a vehicle has anti-lock brakes, you are more inclined to lean in to hear about the benefits associated with the car having anti-lock brakes.

Throughout the presentation, the best way to build rapport is to use carefully crafted questions that show interest and that also position you to conduct some fact-finding.[1]

Instead of "Don't you like X?!" ask, "What do you like the most about X as it relates to being able to [achieve a desired result]?"

Instead of "Isn't Y interesting?!" ask, "What do you find most interesting about Y?"

Instead of "You would use this, right?" ask, "How do you see yourself using this to save money/make money/improve client loyalty?"

When you do that, you achieve the third necessary ingredient for a successful sales presentation; you position yourself to get feedback. The fourth and fifth ingredients are case studies/ testimonials and an impactful closing. You already know the power of a testimonial and can consult with your colleagues for reports of satisfied clients to insert in your presentation. The fifth and final component is covered in "Open with Power and Close the Deal: 8 Scripts to Successfully Conclude a Sales Presentation" in chapter 4.

---

[1] For additional question options, see "Why No One Responds When You Ask 'Are There Any Questions?' and What to Ask Instead" in chapter 3.

OPEN WITH POWER AND CLOSE THE DEAL: 8 SCRIPTS TO SUCCESSFULLY CONCLUDE A SALES PRESENTATION

Have you ever gotten to the end of your sales presentation, and it feels really awkward? You've done a masterful job of explaining the product or service, and without question, you want the business, but you're not quite sure of what to say next or how to say it.

The bottom line is you need to walk away with a signed contract (preferred), an opportunity to send a contract or proposal for the prospect's review, or at least the plan to have a follow-up meeting. Here are eight scripts that naturally conclude your presentation and move the conversation in the direction of any one of those. But just as is the case with any portion of your presentation, these scripts must be practiced; as a matter of fact, practice these closing lines with more focus, frequency, and intention than the rest of your presentation so it's solid. You want them to sound natural. The tone and attitude in your closing words should not be timid or shy; you should sound just as confident (if not more so) in your closing words as you are at any other point in the presentation.

1. Which Two?

"Taking all of your requirements and desires into consideration, these two products will work best for you. Do you want to go with [X] or [Y]?"

If you have presented on two options, then this is an ideal close. The rationale behind giving two alternatives is that the prospect will be more inclined to choose one than turn away both. With this close, you increase your chances of hearing a "yes" to something rather than a "no" to everything.

2. The Guardian

"I'd hate to see [negative consequence] befall your company because you didn't have the right product in place. Are you ready to take the crucial step to protecting your organization today?"

This closing tactic is most effective in those instances where the consequences of allowing the status quo to continue and not buying will actually harm the lead.

3. The Mover

"If all of this sounds good, are you ready to move forward? I can send over the proposal [or contract] right now."

Everyone likes the idea of progress. If you have that kind of lead in front of you who associates getting a proposal or making the purchase with forward momentum, they'll be likelier to take the next step.

4. The Fixer

"Is there any reason, if we give you the product at X price, that you wouldn't do business with our company?"

If the lead answers "no" to this question, then you have indirectly gotten them to agree to the contract. If the answer is "yes," however, you are still in the game and have the opportunity to address objections.

And if the answer is a "no," then follow-up with "If we could find a way to effectively handle [objection], would you sign the contract [by set date]?"

Objections often bring deals to a screeching halt. But in this case, handling the objection is a way of closing the sale. Of course, this depends on your ability to resolve the problem by a given date. But if a fix is possible, getting the customer to commit ahead of time is a smart way of turning a con into a pro.

5. Let's Get Started

"Unless you have [additional] questions or concerns, I believe we're ready to get started."

You're leaving the door open for them to get more information while making it clear where you stand. If you've done your job surfacing and resolving objections throughout the sales process leading up to the presentation, then the lead will answer with something like, "No, I'm good. I think we're ready, too."

6. Talk Numbers

"Let's discuss what the investment for this would look like."

With this statement, you transition the conversation from general, abstract topics like product benefits into the actual agreement. This is not subtle, but if you know you've checked all the boxes with establishing rapport, addressing objections, answering questions, presenting testimonials and case studies as well as the product's/service's benefits, then this is the obvious next step.

7. The Therapist
"Tell me what you're thinking."

To gauge how ready your lead is, say this. If they're looking for the metaphorical pen to sign on the dotted line, they'll usually say so. If they're still unsure, you'll hear some hesitation. This gives you the chance to figure out what's holding them back without trying to close too soon.

8. Ms./Mr. Respect
"We can take as long as you'd like, but I know [you've got another meeting at X time, this call is scheduled to wrap up in Y minutes]. With that in mind, perhaps we should move to the proposal or the actual agreement."

While you don't want to rush your prospect too much, reminding them of the ticking clock gives you a good reason to bring up pricing. Notice this response is framed around their schedule. If they want to continue the conversation you're currently having, you can offer to arrange another meeting.

And with using any of these closing scripts, remember one is no better than the next, and before you use a script, it must align with ...

- your personality;
- the energy of the room; and
- your overall presentation objectives.

IS YOUR CONTENT SUITED FOR A WEBINAR?

First, you must ask yourself if you should even produce a webinar.

Believe it or not, this is a question that most fail to ask before settling on delivering a webinar.

And believe it or not, that's the reason there are so many painfully boring webinars out there. The question that must be answered is "Will this be useful to my audience?"

As such and unfortunately, not all content is best suited for the webinar format. The following would be a good fit for a webinar:

- A detailed examination of a new product that offers new possibilities and/or fresh perspective for solving a problem (a niche topic from a fresh angle)
- A panel discussion of a timely issue or topic in your industry
- A thorough, example-driven "how-to"
- An adaptation of a presentation from a conference or other speaking engagement
- An interview with an industry thought leader

The following would not make for a particularly compelling webinar:

- A minor product release or update
- A news-based webinar with little or no new information/opinion
- A broad, "content thin" webinar on a general topic
- A webinar focusing on a tired idea or concept; remember content is king
- A straight-up sales deck/product pitch

This is not to say you cannot deliver a webinar in any of these instances; this *is* to say that your message would be more effective if delivered via a different medium or in-person.

SHOULD YOUR WEBINAR BE A DEMO, A TRAINING, OR PROFESSIONAL DEVELOPMENT?

Once you determine if your content is a good fit for the online environment,[1] you must examine how those ideas should be presented, as a demo, a training, or as professional development. (This labeling is applicable to both webinars and in-person presentations.)

You label a webinar as a demo when you provide a detailed examination of a new product with new possibilities. This type of webinar is largely focused on pointing and clicking and is typically a pre-sale scenario or a post-sale scenario if it's an update to an existing product. The questions you're answering is "What is it?" "What are the possibilities?" and "What are some problems this might solve with further analysis/discussion?"

You label a webinar a training when you provide a thorough how-to that's meant to instruct and guide one on how to use a product, system, or service. This is typically a post-sale scenario. The questions you are answering is "How does it work?" and "How do I use it?"

Finally, you label a webinar professional development if you are adapting a conference presentation, interviewing an industry thought leader, or facilitating a panel discussion. Any time you advance ideas and expand on the current body of knowledge in an area, then you are offering professional development. When you answer and further the discussion of "why," then you are offering professional development.

---

[1]See "Is Your Content Suited for a Webinar?" in chapter 4 to determine if your content is a good fit for a webinar.

10 BEST PRACTICES FOR CREATING MAXIMUM IMPACT IN YOUR WEBINARS

No matter if you are presenting a demo, training, sales pitch, or professional development, in all instances, your webinar attendees want you to connect, they need your content to make sense, they need you to cut to the chase and not waste their time, and they need you to look and sound alive!

If you don't want to lose too many people along the way and if you want people to retain what you say, then it is imperative that you break up your information delivery into shorter lecture segments while increasing audience involvement throughout the session and varying your use of tools to engage.

Here are seven best practices for creating maximum impact in your webinars.

1. Immediately give the audience a reason to listen.

You grab and maintain audience attention by immediately solving a mystery and giving the audience what it needs, by giving the audience something useful. The script you use to you use to start an in-person session is the same one you use to start a webinar.[1]

Provide ...

- An opening message that clarifies the what and why and that tells them how this session will be useful

- Objectives and agenda items that clearly demonstrate how their time will be spent

- No more than five to seven minutes of content at a time before changing pace and giving participants time to think about what you shared

- Opportunities for processing throughout the session and images and vocal delivery that keep them on their toes.

2. Request their undivided attention.

Giving the audience a reason to listen also aids in keeping multitasking to a minimum, but a proactive move is, at the start of the session and after you have delivered your power intro, to ask for everyone's undivided attention throughout the session. When you make this request, even go so far as to ask everyone to post to the chat "I agree" as a commitment that they will be fully present. It looks like this: "In order for this to be a productive session, I ask for everyone's undivided attention." Simple as that. Follow-up by saying something along the lines of "For those who are unable to give their full attention to the session, then please consider attending at a different time when your schedule allows for a better level of engagement." An additional step is to start the session by requesting everyone close out of other windows and to place their phones at least four feet away from them. That way, if there is an alert that requires their attention, they are close enough to be aware of it, but the phone is not easily accessible, reducing the temptation to get on social media. (Besides, with the planning you'll have put into your session, that webinar is going to be far more interesting than any cat photos they'll find on the 'Gram.)

3. Use the ~5-minute rule of engagement.

There should be no more than five to seven minutes between the speaker talking and participant interaction and collaboration. They should do something so they're not just listening to a talking head. This is not a rigid rule, but it's a good rule of thumb—to speak for no more than five to seven minutes at a time before your audience has an opportunity to engage with the content you presented.[2] This is a shorter amount of time than you would speak in a face-to-face session because you have to compensate for the distance created with you being in the virtual environment where distractions are greater and attention spans are shortened.

4. Make it an experience.

Webinars often do away with hands-on learning, and we tend to focus on delivering information. Instead, have the audience members take the information you provide and engage in tackling real challenges right there in the session. When you make it an experience, you reduce the likelihood of becoming someone who is just trying to get through the information, and you truly engage the audience in a conversation about what the information might mean for them and how they can use and apply it beyond the session. Make a point; give supporting evidence, examples, and stories; then ask a great question[2] that has them adding the content to their knowledge base.

5. Give directives.

Remember we're there to help participants learn, to help them see the usefulness of the information we provide. This involves focusing the audience's attention. Don't be afraid to provide directives like "Write this down" or "Look at this" because 100 percent of the audience is never listening to you at 100 percent capacity 100 percent of the time.

Additionally, if you use breakout rooms, use the chat functionality to provide the directions there, especially if there are multiple steps involved. This allows your participants to maximize their time together instead of wasting precious time, trying to figure out what you wanted them to do/discuss in their breakouts. Provide directions in both written form and verbally. And a pro move is to encourage everyone to take a screenshot of the written directions before they head off to their breakout rooms.

6. Effectively use engagement tools.

Avoid using polls just to shake things up or in an effort to bring some excitement to the webinar. It's okay to use polling questions as a "quiz," but do so in a manner that gets participants excited, changing their current behavior, applying the content to their current circumstances, thinking big picture, or planning for the future.[2] Just as is the case in-person, on webinars, it does not matter the engagement tool you use; what matters is the question you use as the basis of that engagement. Ask a great question, then have them use the annotation tool to circle their answer. Ask a great question, then have them respond via the polling feature.

Ask a great question, then have them chat a three- to five-word response. Limiting chat responses to only three to five words is mutually beneficial. It helps the presenter because it keeps you from having too long of a lull that can come from participants type-type-typing away due to having no parameters placed on the length of the response. At the same time, it takes the pressure off participants from feeling they have to write a tome.

And remember the engagement tools in the platform are not the only engagement tools available to you! You can incorporate into your virtual session stretch breaks or even dance breaks. You can have participants clap. Have them snap their fingers! Have them hold up a pen if they agree or a piece of paper if they disagree with a statement. Have them stand and take one step to the left if they believe X or take one step to the right if they believe Y. Or conversely, have them remain seated but turn their heads to the left or right to signal their responses. There are no correct or incorrect ways to engage your online audience. Get creative!

7. Encourage real-time conversations.

If you do not allow participants to chat with each other or with you, the presenter, then you can make them feel stifled, like they have to sit on their hands and just listen to what you have to say. It can make them feel like you do not believe their ideas are important. Ask participants to choose a participant who's attending the webinar and send a chat to him or her about the biggest ah-ha moment they've had thus far. I have even built into a webinar a break where participants are instructed to take two minutes to email a colleague, using this message stem: "I'm attending a webinar about classroom management strategies, and the most interesting thing I've learned thus far is _____. Remind me to tell you more about it!"

8. Have a system for handling and addressing questions.[3]

Be careful that you do not make people feel stifled by not allowing questions until the very end of the session. Doing so sends the message of "Don't interrupt me; I'm presenting!" It does require that we pay even more careful attention to the time and pacing of the session, but remember … it's about them; it's not about us. If there's a question out there, you don't want people to feel like they have to hold their breaths until the end, which can cause frustration. Direct them to a place in the webinar platform to put their questions, then review it periodically.[3] Let everyone know you will monitor the chat, or better yet, your moderator will monitor the chat, which increases the likelihood of conversations remaining on track.

9. Remember the power of stories.

When we think about presenting, we usually focus on the look of our slides and what we're going to say. But just as important as what we say is how we say it. Are we rambling off stats and pain points? Or are we including stories to further illustrate our points? Our brains are hardwired to respond to stories. Stories are the mental hook that draw in listeners. Do not be afraid to include one when appropriate. Use your own stories or borrow and edit others' stories.

10. Remember looks do matter.

In the online environment, PowerPoint alone has to mimic what we do in the face-to-face environment. Slides serve all the purposes that they do in the physical space and then some. In both settings, they help to focus your audience, but that function is more critical in the virtual presentation space. You can't just turn off the slides and redirect attention to your physical presence. But you need to use slide decks wisely to ensure engagement because the overall aesthetics of a slide sends a message to the brain before we even begin to try to understand the content.

- Use contrasting colors, but remember plain black and white is boring. Use bold visuals, but be selective.

- Fancy, flowery fonts are hard to read; steer clear of them.

- Charts and graphs should not be too complex.

- Provide anchor or progress slides to review what you just covered, preview what you're about to cover, and explain how it all fits together (if necessary).

---

[1]See "The One and Only Way to Ever Start Your Presentation" in chapter 3.

[2]For questions to use that engage your audience, see "Why No One Responds When You Ask 'Are There Any Questions?' and What to Ask Instead" in chapter 3.

[3]For ideas on when to handle questions in your presentation, see "Stop Taking Questions at the End of Your Presentation" in chapter 5.

VIRTUALLY EVERYTHING MATTERS IN A VIRTUAL PRESENTATION

Starting in March of 2020, working remotely and presenting online ostensibly became the norm for many households. Enjoying a much shorter and a far less complicated commute that takes you to the comforts of a home office while attired in a business casual top, pajama bottoms, and fuzzy slippers relaxed some of the business operating rules. However comfortable you get in your WFH routine, one routine with which you cannot afford to get comfortable—if you want to be seen as a respected leader—is how you handle your online presentations.

REAL TALK PRINCIPLE

It's the small details that may escape you but, if ignored, are that upon which audience members will seize and never let go of for the entirety of your webinar.

1. Be aware of your entrance into an online room.

How you "walk" into an online room calls for as much of your attention as how you walk into a physical room. Your entrance into a web conference platform sends a silent message, and the message should not start with "Can you see my video?" or "Can you hear me?"

Always use this rule of thumb: If you can see your video on-screen, then that means your audience can see your video. Conversely, if you see no video of yourself, then it's a safe assumption that your audience does not see you, and you need to engage your camera or ask how to engage it if you don't already know how to do so. But, seriously speaking, prior to getting online, you need to know how to turn on your camera and confirm on your own that everyone can see you.

Also, know how to immediately confirm whether your mic is live or not. Look for a microphone icon; if there is a diagonal line across it, then your mic is not on. That way, you avoid the amateur move of getting into the session wasting time and asking if everyone sees and/or hears you.

2. Know when and how to mute.

Know how to strategically mute and unmute your mic and actually mute it (!) when you have a disturbance in your midst that is out of your control but that may be audible to your colleagues and disruptive to the online meeting. Naturally, do as much as you can in your planning to ensure you are in a quiet space for the duration of your presentation, but we all know things happen; so be prepared by knowing well beforehand where that mute button is located and how to engage it.

3. Stand when speaking.

It can be tempting to sit while you present a webinar—preferably at a desk where you can easily access your notes or where you think you will feel most comfortable; however, there are four big reasons why sitting during this performance is not as effective as standing.

First, standing rather than sitting during your webinar positions you to breathe properly, which gives your voice greater strength and clarity. When you stand while speaking, your naturally good posture can now let the air do the work of carrying the sound of your voice as you speak. You are better positioned to fill your diaphragm, not your lungs, while you speak, and it's having air in your diaphragm that will position your words to float on air and carry; it's having air in your diaphragm that will cause your voice to project and sound confident.[1]

Second, when you stand during your webinars, you are more likely to gesture, which can result in you sounding more comfortable and more confident. However, when you sit to deliver your web-based presentation, you can feel constrained and confined to that limited space, minimizing the amount of gesturing you would do if you were standing; you may even find yourself squirming in your seat or even worse, you may find yourself entirely too lax and casual, giving your performance an entirely too lax and casual feel. Consider this: just as one can "hear" a smile on the phone, one can "hear" gestures, and gesturing while on a webinar "shows" your personality and "shows" you are passionate.

Next, standing keeps you from crossing your legs; more importantly, it keeps both your feet on the ground, which makes it possible for you to perform better at addressing complex questions.

According to body language experts, this has to do with being able easily to go back and forth between the limbic reptilian part of your brain to the neocortex. Having both your feet planted on the floor can help you go between creative thought and highly complex rational thought. (I guess there really *is* something to that "thinking on your feet" phrase, right?)

Finally, standing provides a sense of authority. There is a natural sense of authority that comes with a person who is standing at the front of a room. Now, think about what you relinquish when you sit to give a presentation. If you opt to sit for your presentation, then you are opting to give up your authority. Besides, if you were giving an in-person presentation, would you sit for that? Absolutely not! Claim your authority, and stand for that presentation.

Of course, if you are not physically able to stand, then at a minimum, you are encouraged to sit as close to the edge of your seat as possible or use one of those exercise balls for your seat. Here's why: Doing so forces you to have proper posture, and with that proper posture, you are able to fill your diaphragm with air. This was a trick I learned when I started playing the trumpet in the sixth grade and the baritone in high school. During concert season, our band teacher insisted we sit on the edges of our seats for that reason, and it's a tip that's continued to serve me well when it comes to proper breathing and voice projection.

Quick Note: Don't have one of those standing desks that costs hundreds of dollars? No problem. Use one of my hacks from back in the day: Get a square plastic wastebasket, turn it up-side-down on your desk or any flat surface, place textbooks on the bottom of the wastebasket (which is now the top) until you achieve the right height, then set your laptop atop the stack of books. Set up your light ring so it's illuminating your face, and voila! It's show time!

4. Be aware of and plan for what your will audience see.

I'm not talking about a slide deck here; I'm talking about your attire and your background. If you've ever worked with a realtor to sell a home, you may have heard the word "staging." The point behind staging is simple: You want to position your home so the potential buyer is better able to visualize him/herself in your home. To do so, you declutter and put your home's best foot forward. This may mean tossing some items in storage and bringing in some rented furniture—whatever it takes to make the place pleasing to the eye. The same goes for virtual presentations. Make you and your surrounding pleasing to the eye. Get rid of all the stuff that will be in your audience's field of vision, and wear an outfit that does not take away from your message. You want your audience to visualize itself taking action based on what you're saying, not staring at your wrinkled yet amazingly comfortable v-neck that looks like a u-neck or gawking at all the storage bins, piles of paper, and miscellaneous items sitting around on the floor and against the wall behind you. There is no need to do a massive cleaning or a complete overhaul of your space. Get a preview of what your audience will see by engaging your camera in the platform a day or so before showtime, then move the clutter out of the camera's field of view. (And if you stand for your presentation with your camera positioned just right, then they won't even see that mess on the floor!) The bottom line is it's okay if everything off-camera looks a wreck; just ensure everything *on*-camera looks aesthetically pleasing.

Choose solid warm colors to wear for your online appearances. Colors like teal, cobalt, purple, and coral pop on screen. For men, neckties are your best opportunity to deliver a punch of color. Avoid big patterns as they can appear busy and can easily clash with your surroundings. Also avoid small, tight patterns; they can appear as if they are buzzing on camera, especially small herringbone prints.

When you want your appearance to support you standing out, steer clear of wearing black in the online environment. While it provides for a wonderful slimming effect in-person that some people absolutely love (with me being one of those people!), black attire can make your physique look crushed and shapeless when worn while online.

Don't have teal, cobalt, purple, or coral? The safest route is to wear any solid color.

> I discuss colors to wear and colors to avoid wearing on-camera in more detail in *Show Up and Show Out: 52 Communication Habits to Make You Even More Unforgettable.*

5. Think Texas!

Gesturing online has to take on a "Think Texas" attitude. Everything is bigger in Texas, and everything must be bigger when you gesture online. Lean into your screen to emphasize an idea. Look to the left and the right (and even hold up your hand, placing it horizontally just above your eyebrows as you motion) to mimic being in search of something. Hold up your fingers to count off points. Cup you ear and slightly turn your head to the side to suggest you are listening for a sound. When you are at a distance that's far enough away from your camera to the point your audience can see at least half of your torso— down to the area that is just a few inches above your navel— sparingly, bring up your hands so your gestures can be seen on-camera. Be more animated than you would be in-person because due to the physical distance, it will be just right for the virtual environment.

6. Save your audience (and yourself some embarrassment) from your lack of preparation.

If you plan to show a video during the course of your presentation, then ensure you know how to share your screen or the application *before* the presentation. Refrain from telling the audience you will share a video and that if it doesn't work, then you'll troubleshoot. This is a sure sign you did not prepare, and when it is evident to your listeners you did not prepare, it suggests they were not important enough to you or that your message was not important enough to deserve adequate preparation. Either way, it's not a good look. Again, access the platform beforehand, have someone join you, and share the video to your one-person audience to confirm it can be heard and seen so when you show up for your actual presentation, you are fully prepared.

7. Have a back-up plan for the back-up plan.

I recall once having a tech fail at the very start of a presentation despite having a tech check session the week before and despite arriving to the webinar platform 25 minutes early to check the tech. What did I do? I asked the participants to post to the chat questions they had about the presentation topic that I answered right there on the spot as I simultaneously worked to shift to my back-up plan.

It's great if you can enlist the help of a moderator who can ping you or whom you can ping to handle problems for you in your online session; however, that is not always a possibility. In all instances and especially in those where you have to go it alone without the assistance of a trusted colleague to monitor the chat and attend to other logistics, ensure you have two WiFi sources that are engaged and that are ready to go in the event you lose connectivity. Additionally, have at least two devices logged into the webinar with your slide deck saved to both of them—if you're using a deck—just in case you have to switch from one machine to the second one to continue your presentation because I'm here to tell you—just when you get in the middle of your webinar and it's getting really really good and juicy, your laptop will automatically shutdown to perform an update that is sure to take a minimum of five minutes but that will feel like an eternity. And if you get that gnawing feeling where you *do* detect the possibility there's a problem, think and act in positive terms. Instead of asking "Am I frozen?" say "Please post 'yes' in the chat if you can see and hear me okay." This way, you give a directive for how you need the audience to act, and you learn much more quickly if you need to make adjustments. Don't start sweating if you ask and do not get responses right away; remember there's a tiny delay plus people have to think, open the chat, and type. Stay cool. And if after a few seconds, you get no response, then it's a sure sign you need to troubleshoot; message your moderator if you have one, leave the room and re-enter, engage your second WiFi source, or switch to that second machine you already have set-up. Don't broadcast it, especially considering you will have some who don't even realize there is a problem. Already know what you plan to do before you have to do it, then when you have to do it, just do it.

8. Leave the inconsequential where it is.

Resist the urge to announce that your son just came into the room to ask for your car keys, or apologize for forgetting to silence your ringing phone before the meeting, or acknowledge that your dog barked in the background. First, it is of no conse-quence to the audience that your son made a request for your ride. Second, create a checklist of what you need to do prior to a virtual presentation with one of them being "put phone on silent or in do not disturb mode." (Add to the list "close email and any other applications that may randomly ring, ding, or ping.") Third, the audience may not have even heard your furry little friend in the background anyway, so there's no need to call atten-tion to it in the first place. The point is bringing in commentary that does not add value to your presentation lessens the power and impact of your presentation. We all know you cannot always control your environment when working from home where other members of your household may also be present, going about their daily routines. Simply hand over the keys (or say, "Get an Uber."), silence the phone, or quickly excuse yourself to tend to your chihuahua named Pork Chop. There's no need to announce to the audience what you're doing; simply say, "Please excuse me a moment," and keep the show moving along.

Will your presentation completely fail as a result of any one of these missteps? No, it won't. Does your audience as well as your image deserve everything you can do to give a top-notch representation of your brand and your business? Absolutely. Every. Single. Time.

In *Show Up and Show Out: 52 Communication Habits to Make You Even More Unforgettable,* I provide with twelve practical tools called "Shine Online Tips" that have you confidently showing up in the online environment when you are not making a presentation.

---

[1]For more on filling the diaphragm and voice projection, see "Use a Mic. End of Story." in chapter 5.

REFLECT, REVIEW, AND RESPOND: DO YOU KNOW HOW TO CREATE ABSOLUTELY FLAWLESS PRESENTATIONS?

1. What is included in your presentation plan to guide how you prepare, deliver, and follow-up?

2. What will you do differently in the opening, delivery, and closing of your next sales presentation?

3. How do you know if you should present a webinar?

4. What best practices should you put in place when you present a webinar?

Chapter 5

ENSURE YOU ALWAYS SIZZLE

Chapter 5

ENSURE YOU ALWAYS SIZZLE

It's no secret that trying to attend to every little possibility when making a presentation can be a challenge of seemingly epic proportions. Some of the challenges you face include—but are not limited to—covering large amounts of content, getting audiences members' minds off their devices and everything else and 100 percent focused on you and your presentation, plus checking to ensure you achieved what you came to achieve.

With all of that, it can be hard to ensure you sizzle.

There are so many fine details that, if left unattended, can negatively impact your presentation and your audience's perception of you.

But if you take control of as much as you can, refusing to leave anything to chance, then you are well on your way to delivering a presentation that sizzles.

In this chapter, you will know how to ...

- confidently address any question posed to you
- time your presentation like a pro
- assess at what point to take questions during your presentation
- stay centered and poised when faced with a challenging audience member
- implement pro moves with regard to the use of your notes, the microphone, podiums, and lecterns
- not get rattled by a technological glitch
- expertly handle hiccups as well as instances when people leave your presentation
- make boring content interesting
- prepare to present to an international audience
- avoid getting thrown off your presentation rockstar game

THE 7-STEP METHOD TO EXPERTLY ANSWER ANY QUESTION

You are in the middle of your presentation, and it happens. An audience member asks a question—*that* question—and that "thing" happens to your throat, in your stomach, around your chest, to the palms of your hands…. The number one goal is to look, sound, and aim to be as helpful as possible, especially with those rare questions (or people) that seem like they are meant to rattle you. Here is what you do to expertly take on the toughest of audience questions.[1]

1. Anticipate there will be questions—even the horrible ones you dread!—and prepare by making three lists.

The first list contains the questions to which you know the answers. Write down the questions as well as the answers. The second list includes questions to which you do not know the answers; conduct your research or contact colleagues to get the answers. The third list contains the questions you dread. For those that you dread, know you do not have to answer every question right at that moment. More on that later.

2. Make sure you actually hear the question.

Listen intently—physically and mentally—and do not draw a conclusion or mentally formulate an answer until you hear the entire question. Avoid interrupting the questioner; this benefits both you and the questioner because you show respect by giving him or her the proper time and space to voice the inquiry. It also ensures that you hear the question correctly and are positioned to give an appropriate answer. At times, in the middle of the question, we think we know exactly what is being asked and may begin to nod our heads, mentally preparing a response while not realizing we may completely miss the mark. Then we proceed to cut off the person or immediately begin speaking as soon as the questioner finishes, eager to provide an answer that is ultimately incorrect or partially irrelevant—all because we did not fully hear the question. Don't do that. Allow yourself to hear the question in its entirety.

3. Provide a concise answer and direct the answer to the entire group, not just the person who asked the question.

When responding to any question, do not convey irritation or frustration. Always convey a gratefulness for any question posed, no matter the spirit in which it is asked. No matter what, there will always be the possibility of someone asking a question in an attempt to get you off your game, to call into question your authority or credibility, or to express disdain. (And when it comes to the latter, you really wonder why the person will not simply leave the presentation if he or she is that unhappy, especially if it is in a setting where attendance is not mandatory.)

Even with those questions seemingly meant to derail you, always respond in a way that casts everyone in a positive light.

A little story... Upon publishing her first cookbook, an author and friend of mine received this question from an audience member at a book signing: "Why didn't you include caloric information with the recipes?" This threw her off her game. First, she knew the man. Second, from what she knew of him, she understood he was quite the character (who reveled in trying to trip people up). However, this was not enough to prepare her for her response, which included her apologizing for the omission and explaining her inability to include the calorie count of her recipes. How should she have responded? In the spirit of offering an answer that elevates both the questioner and the speaker, this would have been the better option: "Thank you for your question. It is a great recommendation, and I will take it under advisement when I make revisions or when I release my next book. (pause) Does that answer your question?" This response gives the questioner—and anyone listening—the impression that his input is appreciated. Furthermore, it demonstrates that the author is a true professional who will not feed into an attempt to suggest she or her book missed the mark or fell short in any way. (The hidden message here is "Do not mess with me. I am *not* the one!")

4. Repeat the question so the entire audience hears the question.

If you do not repeat the question, then you run the risk of several people trying to figure out what was asked. This results in disruptive sidebar conversations. Avoid asking "Did you hear that?" before proceeding to answer the question. People will do that— ask "Did you hear that?"—without waiting for or sincerely wanting an answer. In doing so, they subconsciously assume everyone in the audience heard the question, and it gives them permission to proceed as if everyone *did* hear the question. That is not the case. Do not ask if the audience heard the question. Always repeat the question, so you *know* it was heard, then proceed with your succinct answer.

5. Follow-up with "Did that answer your question?"

This shows you care and that you have an actual interest in helping the questioner get his or her answers. If the questioner says your response did not answer the question, then see number six ...

6. Know you do not have to answer every question right at that moment.

If a participant asks a question from that list you dread—a question that is specific to that one audience member or that will require an intricate or particularly detailed explanation— respond as such: "That is a great question, and the answer is quite extensive. So, in the interest of time, please see me after the presentation, and let us discuss at that time." The same goes for anyone who gives you a "no" in return after you respond to a question then ask "Did that answer your question?" Ask that he or she see you afterwards to further discuss. Notice the onus is placed on the questioner to reach out to you. If the question is really important, then you will hear further from him or her. Indicate you will need to research it and get back with him or her; take the necessary contact information, and do indeed follow-up with an answer. But if the questioner does not connect with you after the presentation, then keep it moving!

7. Finally, move on to the next question.

Finish your response by looking to another audience member to avoid getting consumed in a dialogue with just one person. You run the risk of losing the audience's interest if that happens.

---

[1] For guidance on when to take questions during your presentation, see "Stop Taking Questions at the End of Your Presentation" in chapter 4.

NEVER AGAIN GET DERAILED
BY A DIFFICULT AUDIENCE MEMBER

Almost every speaking engagement will present you with a difficult audience member. While this may not be what you want to hear (or read), it is the truth.

This is the person who is cranky for no apparent reason. This is the person who is known by colleagues and coworkers as being difficult and negative 24/7. This is the person with a constant scowl and who frowns upon the site of puppies, rainbows, or flowers.[1] Even if the person says absolutely nothing, this individual is still labeled as a difficult audience member because the aura and affect emanating from his or her body language can be disruptive to your energy and your focus. You subconsciously want everyone enjoying your presentation, and as such, you are inclined to further bend over backwards in an attempt to win over everyone. The fact of the matter is you cannot make 100 percent of the audience 100 percent happy 100 percent of the time, and you cannot control that person, how that person looks, or what he or she says or thinks. However, you *can* control your response to him or her—remain cool, calm, and composed; wonder how many friends the person has; and ignore the person's attitude. (Do not ignore the person. Ignore the attitude.)

Oftentimes, if you are doing a great job with your presentation and others see that, colleagues will address the troublesome person for you. And, even in an audience where no one knows each other, if you are doing an outstanding job, you will have others who recognize that this person is simply being difficult. You may have a situation where that person gets isolated by the majority.

There are two approaches to managing difficult audience members. The first one positions you to handle instances where you know beforehand that the audience may be difficult; and the second one positions you to confidently enter an environment where you assume the best, but you have a plan in the event a heckler makes an appearance.

If you know you are entering a presentation where there is a good likelihood difficult audience members will be present or where you know the topic can lead to challenging conversations, here's what you do:

1. Make a list of the kinds of behaviors you need in order for the session to be a productive one. Call them ground agreements. To create such a list, draw from previous experiences, thinking about what went well and what you would like to see changed. For instance, you may have seen sessions where ...

   • There were challenging behaviors because a participant derailed the session or slowed progress with stuck thinking. Or there may have been sessions where everyone engaged in groupthink, which is equally unproductive.

   • Tensions caused participants to interrupt or talk over each other, and that was not beneficial.

   • Confusion may have overshadowed everything because some participants did not speak up and gain clarity.

- Participants used language that was counter to the culture and energy you needed in a session.

As such, your list of ground agreements might look like this:

- Have an open mind.

- Allow only one person at a time to speak so we all hear each other.

- Ask plenty of questions.

- Always use respectful language.

This list is made in preparation to share it with your audience.

2. After you complete your power intro,[2] ask participants "What do you need in order for this to be a productive session?" Ask them to get into groups of two or three to discuss and create a list of what they need. Allow for a few minutes then ask them to report out. You will likely get responses such as "humor, engagement, activities." Either you or a volunteer writes the list in a place everyone can see it during the entire presentation.

3. Provide your own list that you created beforehand, then ask "Can we agree on this list of agreements?" Once you gain everyone's commitment (or at least the majority of the group) that they will cooperate and abide by the mutually created ground agreements, proceed with your session.

If someone engages in behavior that is counter to any one of the ground agreements, then refer to the list and give a friendly reminder. Do not be afraid to ask an individual to leave if he or she commits repeated offenses, especially if the offenses are overly disruptive to the session.

In the second approach to managing difficult audience members, it calls for you to prepare in a way that keeps the hecklers at bay because it becomes a real issue for a presenter when you are not prepared to address valid concerns that audience members bring up.

The operative phrase is "you are not prepared." Ordinarily, I would write that you must always be prepared, but I realize we are only human. We all have a lot on our plates. I also recognize, especially if you make presentations on a wide array of topics, services, or products, then it is virtually impossible to be an expert on all of them. The challenge is compounded when time is not on your side. In this case, investigating every single angle of a topic is just not feasible.

To combat this issue, choose three to five aspects you will address and on which you will become an expert. Identify those as part of your agenda items or as part of your objectives when you begin your presentation. When you get a heckler who is an expert or who asks a question that is outside of the scope of the presentation or a question that is obviously meant to derail you (try not to think to yourself, "If you are such hot stuff, then why didn't the coordinator of this event get you up here to speak?"), say to the heckler "In the interest of time and focus, I will address only these three components. You and I can certainly have a conversation offline about what you have brought up."

Then put the onus on the heckler to reach out to you: provide your contact information. Do not ask for his or hers. If the point is really important, then you will hear further from him or her; if not, then onward and upward.

Remember if the presenter has not done a good job of providing the audience with useful information or making a wise use of everyone's time, then the majority of the audience will check out. Alternatively, certain audience members will become difficult. The audience members have to "feel" the presenter before they will be cooperative and willing to engage. However, if the presenter has not demonstrated his or her expertise or if he or she has not addressed an elephant in the room, then hecklers will crop up. Therefore, remember this: When frustration comes down, listening goes up.

The best advice is to have an intentional plan for presenting so there are always opportunities for the audience to remain engaged and attentive. Therefore, they will forego trying to derail your efforts. And, as you plan your presentation, constantly be aware of your demeanor and how you come off to others at all times—as if you are on live TV.

REAL TALK PRINCIPLE

Ensure that no matter the disruption, you always give the appearance of being pulled together, unflappable, professional, and polished. Always.

---

[1] A person who appears to have a scowl may not be upset with you, may not dislike your content, and may not even have a scowl. There have been multiple instances where I am presenting my little heart out and catching momentary glimpses of those I have labeled as suspected difficult audience members while thinking to myself, "If you dislike me or my presentation *that* much, then why don't you leave?!" However, what I thought was a scowl from one audience member one time was the face of focused attention, and the audience member actually became an incredible cheerleader of mine! In another instance, the alleged difficult audience member came to me after the presentation to express an appreciation for an instance of graciousness I displayed toward him. Wow—did I get those wrong?!

[2] For more on the power introduction, see "The Way You Have Been Introducing Yourself is All Wrong" in chapter 2 and "The Only Presentation Plan You Will Ever Need Part 2: The Actual Presentation" in chapter 4.

IT'S NOT OKAY IF YOU READ YOUR SLIDES TO THE AUDIENCE

Never read your slides to your audience. So, stop doing it. Right now.

I recall a workshop I once attended where the facilitator stood at the front of the room and read material verbatim from the handout she had provided. I wanted to scream. I walked away having learned nothing I could not have read on my own.

For starters, the audience can read a slide much more quickly than you can read it aloud to everyone. More importantly, you want the audience to pay attention to the words you speak, which should be far more interesting, eloquent, and red-hot than anything you place on a slide. Each slide should contain just enough information to highlight the major points and to support what you say, but it shouldn't tell the entire story.

When a presenter constantly looks up at the projection screen to reference the material or to read it to the audience as opposed to looking at his or her computer screen, it is an unprofessional look. An occasional glance is acceptable because I recognize the room set-up does not always allow for you to reference your computer screen, but these glances should happen sparingly, (And this is where you must ensure you work with the event contact to get the set-up you want and need.[1])

Your eyes should remain focused on the audience. You should talk to the audience, not the projection screen.

Are you checking to see if what is projected is the correct slide? Do not look at the projection screen. You check that by looking at your computer screen.

Are you looking at the projected slide to jog your memory of what you want to say next? Do not look at the projection screen. Look at your computer screen.

Do you want to ensure your media is playing as it should? Do not look at the projection screen. Go to the computer to see if it is properly playing.

You get the idea.

If one thing is for sure, it is that turning to read from the projected slides as opposed to referencing your speaker notes and/or your computer screen is *not* a pro move. Think about this: When you turn to read to the audience from the screen, you are turning your back on your audience to address your audience. You should never do that.

Position your laptop or computer so you are able to easily look at its screen. Remember, it is projecting the same images your audience sees. I also recommend showing your slides in presenter view so your notes are also visible to you while the audience sees only the content on the slides. At the very least, have your notes printed or written out and next to your laptop and other presentation materials. This way, they are easily accessible. The point here is the projected slides are for the audience's benefit, not the presenter's benefit.

---

[1]For comprehensive lists of what to request, see "The Only Presentation Plan You Will Ever Need Part 3: Your Quick and Clean Checklist" in chapter 4.

USE A MIC. END OF STORY.

A speaker should always use a microphone. Many will proudly proclaim their voices carry. That's great for cheering at a sporting event, but it is not a substitute for a microphone in a professional setting. Others possess a fear of the mic, cringing at the thought of their voices being broadcast through speakers. It's time to get past that because when you get on stage, you should assume you have an important message. Everybody is waiting and ready for it, and you should want what you say to be clearly heard.

REAL TALK PRINCIPLE

Your voice, no matter how loud it is, will never be able to take the place of a microphone. Don't try to be a vocal projection hero. Take the mic. Use the mic. Own the mic.

The purpose of using a microphone ensures that no matter where an audience member is seated and no matter where you are standing or in what direction you are facing, everyone hears your voice at the same volume. Without a microphone, even a voice that carries cannot achieve that. Without a mic, you are certain to strain your voice, which is not helpful to you or the audience. Always request well in advance of your event that one be provided for your use.[1] In limited instances, if you are a seasoned orator—depending on the room design, acoustics, audience size, and your awareness of and ability to accommodate audience needs—you may forego using a mic. These instances are *very very* limited.

You should use a mic both to benefit the audience and to protect and preserve your voice. This is incredibly important if you are a professional speaker. And, if you are not a professional, doing so is crucial in those instances when you have to speak at length or when you have to speak repeatedly, delivering multiple presentations on the same day.

Venues that are accustomed to regularly hosting speaking events will likely have lavalier (or lapel) microphones to provide you. Often, these are preferred by most professional speakers as they free their hands for gesturing and/or using a presenter/presentation pointer/clicker to advance their slides. (I have even seen and used one of those nifty headsets you oftentimes see performing artists use during live engagements!) If no lavalier is available (or if the cost is prohibitive), then request a handheld mic. However, use a lavalier mic as often as possible. When you use a handheld mic, your gestures are constrained, and your energy goes down. It does. Just trust me on this one. Insist on a lavalier mic.

What distance should the microphone be from your mouth?

No two voices or mics are exactly the same, but the range of approximately five to six inches from your mouth is standard. Keep in mind mic volumes and room acoustics will differ, so the best way to determine how well you sound on a mic is to arrive at your presentation room at least one hour before your session. Request that a contact from the audio/visual department be there to check your mic levels. Then, ask him or her to be there for the first few minutes of your presentation to make any necessary adjustments because oftentimes, during the actual presentation, your voice will be louder or softer than it was during the mic check.

And if no microphone is present, what is a good way to project your voice so everyone in the room can hear you?

Focus on your passion and personality. Seriously. Think about the last time you discussed a topic that really excited you. What was your energy like? How would you describe your enthusiasm? Was it easy for you to be heard—literally and figuratively? Probably so. When you place yourself in a position to discuss that which matters to you, it is easier for you to speak up and command attention.

After you nail incorporating passion and personality, ensure you always stand up straight, breathe in deeply (but not in a noticeably audible way), and let the air carry your sound as you speak. When you breathe, fill your diaphragm with air, not your lungs. This means your chest rises and your stomach expands; your shoulders should not go up because when your shoulders go up, you are filling your lungs, but it is having air in your *diaphragm* that will position your words to float on air and carry. It is having air in your *diaphragm* that will cause your voice to project. However, if, before speaking, you fill your *lungs* with air, causing your shoulders to go up, then your breath will be shallow and insufficient for projecting. Rather, fill your diaphragm so your abdomen expands. This will help carry your voice.

I have stressed that the speaker should always use a microphone; however, are there instances where you do not have to use one?

If the audience is made up of 15 or fewer people, then no mic is necessary. If you are in a large room, ask for any extra seats to be removed before the start of your presentation. If that is not an option, then politely direct people or have an event contact direct people to sit in a designated area—towards the front of the room where you will be presenting—so you are not as concerned about voice projection.

However, if you know the crowd will be sizable—one that is too large for you to simply use your regular speaking voice and be heard without a mic—then you must insist the coordinator of the event provide you with a microphone. Hands down. It is for both your benefit and the audience's benefit. Your volume naturally reduces over time, so without a mic, the audience's ability to hear you is diminished. This ultimately presents a greater chance of people tuning out. Additionally, you do not want to have to strain your voice as this interferes with your concentration and the quality of your presentation. And, in all honesty, the entire audience—particularly those in the back of the room—cannot hear you when you strain your voice nor is it pleasant to sit and listen to a person shout.

---

[1]For a comprehensive checklist of what to do before your presentation, see "The Only Presentation Plan You Will Ever Need Part 3: Your Quick and Clean Checklist" in chapter 4.

SHOULD YOU STAND ON THE PODIUM
OR BEHIND THE LECTERN?

The answer is yes and no. It's complicated.

Start on the podium and/or at the lectern and end on the podium and/or at the lectern—front and center of the room is your power position—but move away from the lectern as soon as possible for the following three reasons. Bear in mind this is my point of view, and there's no right or wrong answer; it's ultimately up to you to choose what makes the most sense for your comfort level.

1.   Leaving the podium removes an artificial barrier that says to the audience "You're there, and I'm here."

That position, for me, screams "I'm the one with all the knowledge, and you all are here to learn from me." Instead, when you move away from the lectern and/or step down from the podium and get closer to or go out into the audience to present, it sends a much different unspoken message of "I'm not the only one with all the answers. We can all learn from each other." However, if you need to a re-establish a sense of authority, get everyone's attention, regain control of the audience, or make a transition to a new thought, then your lectern or podium awaits you.

2. Leaving the podium creates excitement.

You've seen the crowds go wild when a performing artist leaves her or his position on the main stage to venture out into the audience. I'm telling you—everyone goes mad with enthusiasm! I'm not saying the same will happen in your presentations, but I *am* saying, the energy is different. It feels more electric when you're closer to the action, which is everyone leaning in, listening, wanting every word you have to say. But when you need to bring the excitement down and get everyone back on the same page, ready for a slower pace or a more serious thought, then do not hesitate to get back to that lectern or podium.

3. Not being on that island makes you, the presenter, feel less alone, and it makes the audience feel less alone.

You feel more united; it closes the gap and says "We are all in this together." But the island is always there if you feel you need to return to it to regroup or reset your energy.

After all this, you may say "But I need to be able to see my laptop while I present!"

This is very true.

When I have the latitude to make specific set-up requests, I consistently state I will not use the lectern and that I need my laptop positioned so I can see it all times when I'm presenting. Sometimes I get what I want. Other times, I don't. What do I do when I don't? I wait for no one to make it happen for me. I make it happen for myself.

REAL TALK PRINCIPLE

Do not cross your fingers and hope you get the set-up you want for your presentation. Either ask for it outright or step up and make the set-up happen yourself.

I arrive to the room early enough to reconfigure things myself. I have my own connectors, clicker, power cords... unplugging and rewiring everything to my liking. The thing is, though, you have to remember to put things back the way they were for the next presenter and ensure you collect all your possessions! (I have left behind more cords in more venues than I care to count.)

Remember to start on the podium and/or at the lectern and end on the podium and/or at the lectern, but do not stay there for the entire presentation.

Quick Note: You may have noticed I've used both the words "podium" and "lectern." They are not one in the same. You stand on a podium; you stand behind or at a lectern.

HOW TO EXPERTLY HANDLE A TECH FAIL

In short, if it's broken, don't mention it.

Well ... you can mention it (and in some instances, you probably should!); just don't keep mentioning it.

One of my friends and colleagues shared with me how all she could remember from a presentation she attended once was how the speaker constantly spoke of her inability to get the technology to work. Over and over again, she drew attention to what wasn't properly functioning and how annoyed she was while waiting to figure out the technology. While the actual presentation topic was interesting, all my friend could remember was the bungles.

REAL TALK PRINCIPLE

Remember, your audience will remember
what gets your attention.

And the challenge with technology is no matter how much you plan and prepare, it can be glitchy.

When you have a tech fail, do not make a big deal of it. If it fits with your personality, add some levity to the moment; tell a joke about an issue you've had with your smartphone or your work computer or make light of the situation. I recall a colleague who, at the start of a faculty development workshop, would tell professors, "Because this is a technology session, something will go wrong, and when it does, I want you to clap." And being the good students they were and because technology likes to meet expectations, the professors would clap and laugh right on cue when there was a tech hiccup!

Come prepared with a story to tell that connects with your presentation topic and that fills the time as the tech gets fixed. One of my fellow speaker friends did this, and the audience thought it was an official part of his presentation!

If you have factored in a dramatic element that is most effectively created only if your technology is fully operable, then purposefully stall with a one-minute conversation, e.g., instruct your audience to have a one-minute conversation with a neighbor about what they've learned thus far and a question they still want answered. Naturally, the conversations can go for longer than a minute. Take note of the questions and immediately answer them or save the answers for later. It buys you time while the tech gets up and running.

Finally, and most importantly, know your content well enough to keep moving without the tech because there's nothing you can put on a slide that's more dynamic, more interesting, or more engaging than you.

(Covering this topic reminds me of my wedding day. When I entered the sanctuary, ready to walk down the aisle and meet my oh-so handsome prince who was standing at the altar, looking dashing as ever, the second I saw the flower arrangements that were waiting to greet me at the end of my journey as a single woman, I wanted to absolutely scream. I. Mean. SCREAM. Those arrangements were NOT—UNEQUIVOCALLY NOT—what I had envisioned and that I had described to the florist. Let me tell you…I seriously wanted to throw down my own bouquet [which I really liked and still have to this day!], snatch up those flowers in a Herculean grip, and hurl them out a window somewhere! But. I couldn't. You see, no one would have remembered how gorgeous my husband looked or how angelic I appeared in my gown. All they would have remembered was what got my attention, which, in a moment of lost self-control, would have been me going seriously mad on those floral arrangements!)

Again, your audience will remember what gets your attention. Don't let the tech take over; leave only good memories with them.

WHAT TO DO IF YOU EXPERIENCE A MISSTEP IN THE MIDDLE OF YOUR PRESENTATION

When you have a hiccup in your presentation, avoid sounding an alarm. Avoid letting it be known to the audience that you committed a misstep by making some big announcement such as "I didn't mean to do that" or "I'm sorry; I messed that up" or "I won't be able to get to that" because there's really no valid point in doing so. Think about a newscaster who has a misstep; she does not so "Oh! I meant to say X." She just says what she meant to say. He doesn't exclaim "Oops! That was supposed to be ..." He simply gives you the correct version of the story.

If you call attention to the mistake, ask yourself why you're doing that. Do you want to ...

1. further bring it to your attention that you've done something wrong or that you've omitted content? (Why would you do that? It doesn't add shine to you or your presentation! Besides, no one is the wiser if you have a hiccup as long as you don't say anything about it.)

2. put the audience on notice that you made a mistake? (There may be people in the audience who didn't even detect the error. Again, why call everyone's attention to it? Doing so brings no value.)

3. convey to the audience that you're rattled? (Your audience wants a poised and confident speaker, not a rattled one. They

hope and assume you have prepared to the best of your ability and want to see you do well. Telling them you're rattled
or off your game is of no benefit to anyone.)

If you have a hiccup, say nothing, quietly recover, and move on.

SOMEONE LEFT YOUR PRESENTATION!
WHAT DO YOU DO NOW?!

Sometimes you get those audience members who give you nothing. Some will just sit there and look at you. There's no smile. No shift in their seat. No nothing. And there are those other instances where someone will leave the room. And that can worry you, too. But don't let it.

Some may be perfectly fine with sitting there in a state of calm, watching your presentation unfold. And especially, if they stay throughout your presentation, this is a sure sign that they are engaged and wanted to hear what you had to say. Their lack of emotion? Don't let it bother you. Or if that admonition isn't enough, shift your gaze to lock eyes with another audience member who has a more pleasing countenance.

But what do you do if the opposite happens? What do you do if someone doesn't just sit and stare at you, but instead, that someone gets up and leaves?!

Do not take it personally. The exit may have absolutely nothing to do with you or your presentation.

- They may have a call they need to take.
- They may have received a message from their boss that needs their attention stat.

- They may be going to visit the facilities or attend to some other personal matter.

- They may have another meeting they need to attend and must leave your session early in order to be on-time to the other engagement.

- They may have accidently double-booked themselves and just realized they are supposed to be elsewhere at that very moment instead of in your presentation.

- They may have entered your session on accident and meant to attend the session next door.

- They may have incorrectly read the session description or formed an inaccurate idea of what the session would cover.

It could be anything.

And even if they leave for none of those reasons (not that you would necessarily know), realize your message may not be the one they need at that moment, and that's okay.

REAL TALK PRINCIPLE

Your message may be all that and a bag of chips, but some listeners may need something with a different crunch to it. And that's okay.

It does not mean your presentation does not have value. It just means it does not hold value for that particular individual in that particular moment. This goes for any presentation you deliver; while your title and description may have been well-written and widely publicized, when you get into the meat of your delivery, your message may not be 100 percent meant for everyone assembled at the very minute you deliver it.

But what if you see a mass exodus? (I've been in countless presentations and have *never* seen this happen, but let's just go out on a limb here.) If you see a large number of people making their way out the door, unless you've gone over time and they are hustling out to the next conference breakout session, be honest with yourself, and do the work of re-examining your content and your audience. Double-check to ensure your presentation answers questions the audience has and that it solves problems that plague them.

Finally, work hard to avoid letting your power go out the door with anyone who leaves your presentation, and do not let your energy get sucked out by audience members who do not wear their emotions on their sleeves. In a room of 100 people, if you have two who leave and three who give you blank stares, you still have 95—count them … 95!—who are giving you their attention. Focus your efforts on the majority, and don't worry about those who are seemingly not aligned with the verve you want to see. What you do now is redirect your efforts toward those who are still assembled and interested, those who are deserving of your message, and give the 95 percent what they came to get!

THE PROBLEM WITH ASKING "HOW AM I LOOKING ON TIME?" AND HOW TO FIX IT

Here's what to do so you never utter those dreaded words "How am I looking on time?" You should always know the timing of your presentation, and you should never have to guestimate how many minutes you have remaining. You are the master of this production; you are in control of this show. You should know what's happening at all times, especially as it relates to making an impression on your audience.

Having to ask someone how you're looking on time may be perceived by the speaker as a move to make you appear human, but what it actually communicates is you did not properly plan. You can ask "How am I looking on time?" but do it silently as a reminder to yourself to check the clock to ensure you are respectful of everyone else's time.

You must practice.

Winging it will always have you asking "How am I looking on time?" which is an amateur move; it interrupts the flow of your presentation and sends a signal to your audience that you may very well be winging it. When you practice full-out at least three times as if your audience is right there with you, you can make adjustments to your pace, and you know what your timing looks like.[1]

There's no rule that's been carved in stone, dictating you follow your script to a "t."

Let the vibe from the audience steer the direction in which you go and dictate for how long you speak at any given time. However, do not take all direction from the audience. Know what message you must get across, and make it happen. Avoid, at all costs, allowing the audience to derail you.[2] All that matters is that you maintain audience engagement and that you conclude your presentation on time. It is not absolutely imperative you cover every single point that you planned to cover, especially if you are running the risk of going over time. The audience does not know or feel that they missed out unless you make a big announcement that you failed to cover an item. So, what does that mean? Simple. If you need to jettison some material to ensure you are respectful of time, do not make a big announcement (or even a little one) that you failed to cover an item.[3] Just quietly move on.

Finally, to have absolutely no doubt where you stand when it comes to time, provide your own clock.

Either have one of those small travel clocks with you as part of your presentation supply kit[4], or discreetly check the time on your phone. (This means you have set-up your presentation space beforehand to ensure your phone is already easily accessible. And ensure it's a discreet check. Just tap the screen to awaken the time display. There's no need to pick it up or to broadcast that you are checking the time.)

Before you begin speaking, glance at the time and know you have 10 minutes to talk. When it feels like 10 minutes have elapsed, casually make your way back over to your clock to glance down at it for confirmation. It should not appear as if you are looking at your phone but rather that you are consulting your notes or information on your laptop. Of course, if you use your phone, then ensure you resist the temptation to check a new text message or a social media alert that may have come through. Just saying…

But why not just glance at your wristwatch?

I think you know the answer to that. Have you ever been with someone who did that while you were talking? How did that make you feel?

Right.

Don't do that to your audience.

---

[1]For details on exactly how to practice your presentation full-out, see "Why You Get Nervous Before a Presentation and the Expert Practice Strategy Guaranteed to Change That" in chapter 1.

[2]For how to address difficult audience members, see "Never Again Get Derailed by a Difficult Audience Member" in chapter 4.

[3]Get more on what to do in "What to Do If You Experience a Misstep in the Middle of Your Presentation" in chapter 4, and find out what to do with extra material you do not get to cover in "3 Ideas for What to Do With All That Content That You Cannot (and Should Not) Squeeze Into Your Presentation" in chapter 3.

[4]See "The Only Presentation Plan You Will Ever Need Part 3: Your Quick and Clean Checklist" in chapter 4.

STOP TAKING QUESTIONS AT THE END OF YOUR PRESENTATION

There are three options available to you for when you take audience questions: throughout your presentation as they randomly arise, at designated points in the presentation, or at the very end. While I have a distinct preference—as you can tell from the title of this section—read on to find out which is the right one for you.

And bear in mind that taking questions at the end is not an absolutely terrible thing to do; it's just that it's … well … old. It's what's expected, it's not audience-centric, and it does not positively impact your overall presentation success.

Taking Questions at the Very End

Pros: You are positioned to deliver all your content uninterrupted. Plus, you do not have to worry about losing your train of thought or getting derailed by a question to which you do not know the answer.[1]

Considerations: Bear in mind that if an audience member has a question at minute 10 of a 60-minute presentation, then he or she has to sit and wait until the very end to get an answer. Getting an answer to that question may be integral to the participant understanding the rest of the presentation and can, therefore, hamper engagement with content that's presented after the 10-minute mark. Additionally, if you wait until the end to take questions, you have to answer them out of context, creating a challenge for you, the presenter, with trying to recall at what point in the presentation you were that sparked the query then simultaneously formulating an answer.

Quick Note: With this option, ensure you allot at least one-sixth of your total presentation time for questions, e.g., if you have one hour to present, then allot 10 minutes for questions.

Taking Questions at Designated Points

Pros: This gives you the opportunity to regularly check for understanding, plus the audience does not feel the constraint that comes from having to wait until the very end to get answers to their questions.

Considerations: You must plan for this. If not done well by a thoughtful speaker who has incorporated appropriate transitions before and after the Q&A segment, then it can make the presentation seem choppy. To avoid a lull, you must not assume there *will* be questions from the audience.

Taking Questions Throughout

Pros: This makes the presentation more of a conversation, and it's an audience-centric strategy. When you say in your opening words "Stop me at any time with your questions," it brings a smile to listeners' faces. They immediately they know do not have to wait until the end, but instead they know they will receive real answers to real problems in real time. This strategy is my preference.

Considerations: It requires a skilled speaker who is comfortable with interruptions and who is ready to think on his or her feet. You have to pay attention to your time because if you're not careful, you can find yourself scrambling to get through your content with only a few minutes remaining.[2] However, I find answering audience questions is often more valuable than any prepared content I have. And bear in mind if someone asks a question that you know is personal in nature and/or that would not be of great interest to the rest of the audience, ask the questioner to see you after the presentation to discuss.[3]

---

[1]See "What to Do if You Lose Your Train of Thought" in chapter 1 and "The 7-Step Method to Expertly Answer Any Question" in chapter 5.

[2]See "The Problem with Asking "How Am I Looking On Time?" and How to Fix It" in chapter 5.

[3]For more on how this is done, see "Never Again Get Derailed by a Difficult Audience Member" in chapter 4.

WHAT YOU NEED IS SOME ZHUZH: 10 BIG IDEAS FOR WHEN YOU HAVE TO DELIVER THE SAME (OR REALLY BORING) CONTENT OVER AND OVER AGAIN

How do you add energy to a presentation when you it's the exact same material you have to deliver multiple times or when it's black-and-white, technical, or dry content that needs to be more interesting? I've got you covered!

First, do not feel like you are resigned to delivering the content exactly by the book. There's nothing stopping you from adding a moment of levity or riffing off a comment from the audience. Now, let me be clear: If you are expected to present the information in its entirety or in a certain sequence, then do that. But do not do so at the expense of losing your audience.

And, yes, there is some material that, by its very nature, leaves little room for fun. But put forth the effort. Take a detour—a temporary departure from what their brains expect, a departure from a somber or intense tone—and subsequently increase the likelihood that audiences remember your content, that they actually enjoy it, and that they enjoy you as a speaker.

To start, avoid taking yourself too seriously, your audience too seriously, or your content too seriously, and add some zhuzh.

Zhuzh can be a number of things, but in short, it's what makes you and your presentation stand out and what makes it memorable. It's the integration of your personality and is what has people talking about your presentation (in a good way!) long after it's concluded.

You insert zhuzh by...

1. adding a personal observation in relation to the content: "When I read this, it made me think of/reminded me of ..."

2. displaying an outrageous facial expression: If you make a statement that is surprising, questionable, or interesting, pause to ensure you have the audience's attention with all eyes on you, then give them the rest of the story with your face.

3. inserting an anecdote: Tell one of your own as it relates to the content or borrow one you've heard or read elsewhere that you believe is a perfect fit for the moment. One of my favorite resources for this is *99 Inspiring Stories for Presentations* by Barry Powell.

4. plugging in some self-deprecation: "Here's what would have happened if this had been me..." And if you're clumsy, uncoordinated, rhythmically challenged, and completely out of touch with pop culture like yours truly, then this is an easy one!

5. peppering in personal jargon: We all have favorite sayings or phrases unique to our personalities, and I have loads of personal jargon. At times, I will make a reference to myself

that I need to "get on the good foot," which means I need to get my act together to finish a project or to take care of some business and I need to get it together fast! Or when I want to reiterate the veracity of a point, I may say "That's the actual factual." Once during a conference break-out session on how to deliver great sales presentations, I asserted the participants would leave the session feeling like they are "the bomb dot contract" (as opposed to "the bomb dot com"—get it … sales pros … contracts? Ha!) Finally, if I'm on the verge of getting angry, I'll describe myself as "nearly coming unglued" or "unhinged," which must be said with an exclamation point! On a somewhat related note, I'm thoroughly convinced I was the first person to ever say "It is what it is." Back in the summer of 2005 or so was the first time I uttered it to a sorority sister while driving to a meeting, and after that, it took off and ended up in regular rotation. But I digress …

Dig out your favorite sayings, and add them to your script. Your audiences will love it.

Bear in mind you do not have to be the only source of zhuzh. It can also come from a number of other sources. Options outside of yourself include …

1. having fun with the English language: Use alliteration to make your message more magical or assonance to insert intrigue and interest into your information. [Did you see what I did there?!] Offer a creative play on words with

puns. Use repetition such as "roam through the roses, dance through the daisies, or tiptoe through the tulips" or "walk that walk and talk that talk." Whatever you do, have some pun with it!

2. referencing current events: This is particularly effective in making material relevant and keeping content fresh, especially when it's the same content you have to present over and over again. Scan the week's headlines, and conduct online searches for happenings that have a connection to your topic.

3. sharing song titles or lyrics that align with a point you want to make: One of my top activities to illustrate how to build confidence is to first ask participants to each share the title of their favorite song, the one that makes them feel on top of the world. We then discuss how listening to your favorite song playing in your head, then walking to the beat of it can instantly give you a confidence boost. If you want participants to explore a feeling or a mood as it relates to your presentation, you can do the same by asking them to shout the names of songs that make them feel a certain way or that create a certain mood for them. You can also incorporate actual music by having participants engage in one-on-one or small group discussions during your presentation, and announce that when time is up, they will hear music. (Keep track of time, and play a pre-selected universally-appealing song.) And if you're feeling bold, you may go so far as to have folks dance a momentary jig!

4. changing how you ask questions and how participants respond to questions: Start by no longer asking "Are there any questions?" then see "Why No One Responds When You Ask 'Are There Any Questions?' And What to Ask Instead" as well as "How to Ensure You Reach Everyone in the Room" in chapter 3.

5. providing a cartoon: Do you have a favorite strip now or from back in the day? Or if not, then just conduct a Google search. Let's say I'm presenting on the "thrilling world" of watching paint dry; I'd simply conduct a search for "cartoon strip about drying paint."

REAL TALK PRINCIPLE

Whatever you do, make your presentation a memorable experience for both you and your audience.

MAKE SURE YOU SPEAK THEIR LANGUAGE: BEST PRACTICES FOR PRESENTING TO AN INTERNATIONAL AUDIENCE

Most native English speakers do not speak a second language, including yours truly. (As a result of having taken multiple courses in both high school and college, I dabble in Spanish well enough to barely get by in a Spanish-speaking land, but I'm by no means fluent.) As a result, native English speakers have little to no empathy with an audience that's filled with participants who don't also speak English. It's a different experience—that's for sure. Imagine putting the shoe on the other foot and listening to someone who speaks too quickly; who makes cultural references you don't understand; or who turns to read from the screen, precluding you from being able to read their lips or properly hear the speaker. (If you are guilty of the latter in front of *any* audience—international or not—then it's imperative you review "It's Not Okay If You Read Your Slides to the Audience" in chapter 5.)

Some of the challenges international audiences have when you present include, but are not limited to, the speaker engaging in the following:

- Speaking too quickly

- Poorly articulating your message

- Using too many compound, complex, and/or compound complex sentences and/or phrases

- Using jargon and making references to sports, politics, art, music, pop culture, and everyday life that may have no meaning for the audience

- Using figurative language, humor, and slang that can cause confusion

- Unintentionally hiding your mouth from the audience, precluding them from being able to read your lips, which can greatly aid in comprehension

As such, when you present to an international audience, keep the following in mind:

1. Speak at a rate that is approximately 30 percent to 50 percent slower than your normal rate. (We speak at a rate of 140 to 180 words per minute. To achieve a more accurate assessment, record yourself speaking for one minute, use a speech-to-text app to get a word count, then do the math to slow down your speed.)

2. Take longer pauses at the commas, ends of sentences, and paragraph changes.

3. Use simpler words as well as shorter sentences.

4. Place more emphasis on key words.

5. Do not allow the ends of words to drop as native English speakers tend to do; ensure you pronounce the end consonants in every word.

6. Keep your face pointing towards your audience as often as possible.

7. Synchronize your words and your accompanying visuals as closely as possible.

8. Limit the number of words on each slide.

9. Maintain eye contact with everyone in the room.[1]

10. Constantly monitor the faces in the audience; if you detect looks of confusion, then they are sure indicators you need to double-down on your efforts with attending to numbers 1 through 9.

But when you read through the list, quite frankly, these are best practices you would do well to always employ, not just with an international audience. And when you do this—incorporate these steps on a consistent basis with all audiences—when you find yourself in front of an international audience, it's much easier to put these measures in place.

---

[1]For more on making eye contact with everyone in the room, see "The Body Language That's Required to Own the Room" in chapter 2.

20+ MISTAKES YOU DON'T EVEN REALIZE YOU'RE MAKING ... AND HOW TO FIX OR AVOID THEM ALTOGETHER

1. Never say to the audience "Come on! You can do better than that!" or any statement along those lines.
You usually hear this after a presenter greets the audience and receives a less than enthusiastic greeting in return; oftentimes the presenter will insist—jokingly or otherwise—on telling the audience it can do a better job of returning or responding to his or her greeting.

a. Unless you have rockstar status, you have not done anything to get people hyped. When you say "Come on! You can do better than that!" in response to the audience's greeting, you immediately suggest the audience is inadequate or that they are responsible for setting the tone and creating the energy. Again, all you have done is taken to the mic. When you say "hello" and get a lackluster reply, remember you have yet to do anything to get the crowd excited.

b. Do not rely on the audience to get you excited. Never make the audience responsible for making you feel welcome and wanted. Get yourself pumped by thinking of what value you will bring to rock the house! Think to yourself "Okay. You aren't excited now, but wait until you get a load of this presentation!" Almost approach it as a challenge; you want to deliver a presentation that will result in a marked and positive contrast in the audience's energy from when you start versus when you finish.

c. Greet everyone, accept the greeting you get in response, then set out to totally wow the crowd. It's at *that point* you will see audience excitement go through the roof!

2. Never speak with your back to your audience.

Your voice carries in the direction in which you are facing. If you are not facing your audience when you speak, then naturally, your audience cannot hear you. You may ask "What if I'm using a mic?" It's not a pro move to ever speak with your back to your audience. Even if you're using a mic, always face your audience when you speak.[1]

3. Never say ...

a. "Did everyone hear that?": Repeat yourself. If you feel the need to ask that, then that is an obvious sign you need to restate what you said or repeat the question or comment posed by an audience member. Besides, 100 percent of the audience is never listening at 100 percent capacity 100 percent of the time—no matter how dynamic the speaker may be.

b. "Everybody knows what 'X' is, right?" or "Everybody knows who 'Y' is, right?" or any other similar rhetorical query: It sounds like anyone who does not know X or Y is inadequate, ill-informed, or not in-the-know. No one ever wants to feel that way. However, questions of that nature leave that impression. Seldom will anyone speak up and say he or she does not know "X" or "Y" but will suffer in silence, wondering if he or she is alone, or will forego the suffering and instead will out-right dismiss what comes next out of not having the inclination to ask for additional information. If you feel compelled to ask that, then again, it is a sure sign you need to spell it out. And avoid saying "I'm sure you all know…" for the same aforementioned reasons. Just state it.

c. "You probably don't know this …" or "Most people don't realize …": There may be people in the audience who *do* know or who *do* realize. So, instead of assuming—and verbalizing this assumption—people are not knowledgeable, rhetorically say "Did you know…?" then give the rest of the story. Avoid telling the audience it is not in the know.

4. Never let the audience start a conversation or any other activity without you giving clear directions.

Provide the directions for the conversation or activity at least two times with one of those instances being in writing. Never let conversations or activities begin without letting everyone know how much time is allotted for said conversation or activity.

5. Never begin speaking until you are standing completely still and until you have everyone's attention.

If you need help getting everyone's attention after asking "May I have everyone's attention?" and not receiving it, …

a. say "Clap once if you can hear my voice," then also clap yourself; then say, "Clap twice if you can hear my voice," then clap two times (you will hear more people in the audience join you at this point); then says "Clap three times if you can hear my voice," and clap three times.

b. use a bell. If there are conversations underway because you directed them to take place, then ring the bell once and only once to get everyone's attention. (Do not ring it multiple times; that is annoying.)

c. call for everyone's attention with "May I have your attention?" then silently stand at the front and center of the room with a smile on your face. Do not say another word, and do not continue with your presentation. Everyone will get the message that you have no plans to talk over people, and in short order, many will catch on and will tell others to be quiet.

d. Start you next statement with only the first few words. Repeat those same few words three or four times until the audience quiets down. For instance, if conversations are going, you need everyone's attention, and the next thing you plan to say is "Our next agenda item is planning for tech fails in your session," say "Our next agenda item—. Our next agenda item—. Our next agenda item is..." Everyone will eventually get the idea that you are ready to move on.

6. Never call on an audience member to give information without alerting the audience member beforehand.

This is different from calling on an audience member to share information that was just discussed with other colleagues as part of an activity; in this instance, all are similarly situated. However, when you call on an audience member out of the blue to give a response without allowing for any preparation, it unfairly catches the person off-guard. This demonstrates a lack of audience awareness. Always ensure audience members are adequately prepared before you call on any one of them to speak in front of everyone.

7. Never say "Do you want to share?"

a.   It is a close-ended question and, therefore, gives the person the option to say, "No." (I have seen this happen!)

b.   It makes you sound weak.

c.   Instead, say any one of these:

- "I need X number of volunteers to share Y."

- "I know Beth and Ron have done Z. Please share your experiences."

- "Please take two minutes to discuss X in groups of three. Select someone who will share your findings with the larger group."

- "I will now pass the mic to Meg." And if you opt for this one, then remember number 6 above.

8. Never pose a question to the audience within the first few minutes of your presentation then call on an individual to bravely answer it in front of everyone before you have provided substantial substantive content.

a. You may not have provided enough information for a person to have a fair chance to come to a correct conclusion.

b. Remember, it feels safer to answer a question in front of a small group of listeners than it does to answer a question in front of a room full of people.

c. Your first question should be one where audience members first engage with each other, discussing possible answers to the question. Only after this occurs should you call on a participant to offer answers and remarks to the rest of the audience.

9. Never call on a participant to answer a question to which the answer serves as a basis for understanding an integral part of your presentation without you also providing the answer.

a. Let that person offer an answer.

b. Thank him or her regardless of whether the audience member's answer was correct or incorrect.

c. Ensure you provide the definition you need everyone to have.

10. Never apologize for interrupting/stopping conversations that must come to an end anyway in order for you to continue with your presentation.

You have heard people say it before: "I'm so sorry I have to stop your conversations." Avoid saying that; it's not cute. Sure, you are appreciative of everyone diving in and engaging, but do not apologize for having to continue with your presentation; that is what people came to hear. Simply thank the audience for the robust discussions, note how much you enjoyed the energy surrounding the conversations, and move on with your presentation.

11. Never position the audience to engage in too much multitasking.

Here is a true story: I once attended a luncheon where the presenter, all in the space of less than a minute, told the audience to complete the evaluation, announced the date of the next luncheon, told us to get ready for a prize drawing, and instructed everyone to clap in appreciation for the local restaurant that provided the food.

Do we complete the eval?

Jot down the information for the next luncheon?

Listen for the names of the drawing winners?

Or put down our pens to give applause?

If you must move the event along, then ensure you have a logical order for what you want the audience to do. It is hard to simultaneously write and listen, so save the writing for the end. Giving applause is quick and easy, so make that first. To that end, clap, draw for prizes, announce the next luncheon date, then ask everyone to complete the evaluation.

12. Never say "Without further ado..."

A definition of "ado" is "fuss, especially about something that is unimportant." When you say, "Without further ado," you are ostensibly saying "Let us move on so we no longer have to hear [insert speaker's name] continue to fuss about something that is unimportant."

13. Never look anything short of polished and professional.

The list could go on forever as to what to do and what not to do in this area. Here are a few:

a. Visit the presentation place at least two hours before show-time so you are familiar with the room. A visit the day before is even better.

b. Start your setup no later than 45 minutes to one hour before show time, especially if you will use technology as part of your presentation. (Not sure if you can gain access to the room that early? Ask! Let the organizer know this is part of your practice for ensuring you are set and ready to give a great performance. What organizer will turn you down with that rationale?![2] However, I realize with conference breakout sessions, timing can be tight, so if you can't gain access that far in advance of your session, find out exactly when you can get in there and be ready to make a move.)

c. Do not needlessly point out inconsequential errors or problems. When you call attention to errors or missteps, people will remember those more than they will remember occurrences that went well during your presentation. If there is a problem with the technology, just handle it.[3] If a problem arises, just move on. If a functionality fails to work properly, find a work-around. If you misspeak or say the wrong word, do not say "Oops" or "I'm sorry. I meant to say…" Simply stop yourself and say what you intended to say. The audience will be very clear about what you are doing without you calling any further attention to your slip-up.[4] Do not make a big announcement or get all out of sorts. A little story to illustrate this…Once when I arrived at my conference presentation room, I noticed the left side of my slide deck's projected image was slightly fading. The other side duplicated a portion of the far right side of the slide. It was not a huge distraction, and it did not significantly interfere with the audience's ability to see and understand my slides (since I tend to use a lot of large images and few words). However, it was noticeable, nonetheless, especially on slides with full text where I was demonstrating examples of scripts to use when starting your presentation. At about the halfway point, a participant called attention to the malfunction in the projector to which I replied "Yes, I noticed that prior to the start of the presentation; however, the event contact informed me the venue was not able to fix this, and I hoped by not saying anything about it to you and by acting like nothing was wrong that none of you would notice it. I see that approach did not quite work the way I planned it." Everyone got a good laugh out of it, but everyone got it, too. It was a presentation on presentation skills, and they received an unintended lesson, which was never look short of polished and professional even if there is a glitch. (Interestingly enough, the clicker that was provided at that conference did not work either. What did I do? I had my own clicker with me and was able to use that instead. So, another lesson here is to always be prepared with back-up plans. And speaking of clickers ...)

d. Do not point the clicker at the screen to advance slides. (You know you have seen it. The presenter lifts and points the clicker at the projection screen, then clicks the button to advance the slide as if the clicker is a remote control from back in the day where, in order for it to work, you had to point it directly at the TV with the rabbit-ear antenna.)

- First, it is not the screen that controls the clicker's functionality; to that end, it would make more sense to point the clicker at the laptop or the computer.

- But second, and more importantly, it is not necessary to do either one.

- Simply discreetly click the clicker to advance your slide without a lot of movement of the arm or hand. Think of the bank teller pressing the button under the counter to alert law enforcement there is a robbery in progress.

Yeah. Like that. If all of a sudden, the clicker malfunctions, trust me—pointing it at the projection screen and pushing the button as hard as possible will not fix it nor will it make you look like a pro. If you have problems with your clicker, check to ensure that the transmitter is correctly inserted in your laptop or computer, change the batteries, replace the clicker with another one, or manually advance your slides.

e.   Avoid audible swallowing. When you speak at length, saliva builds in the mouth, prompting you to need to swallow. To avoid the offensive noise that people sometimes make when they swallow while speaking, practice discreet swallowing. You do this by being intentional. Know if you are indeed guilty of this when you speak, then ensure you do *not* make the offending sound that results from releasing your tongue from the back of your teeth and/or the roof of your mouth. Silently release your tongue for a virtually undetected swallow.

14. Remember your voice is part of the presentation.

Just as your attire or your slide deck is an extension of your presentation and can impact the impression people have of you and your overall performance, the same goes for your voice. It is part of the presentation package as well. A voice that drones on or that has no inflections can make for your listeners a painful experience. And, unfortunately, the richness and robust nature of your content may not be enough to move listeners past a voice that sounds disinterested or from a speaker who sounds disconnected from the audience.

To work to have a more animated voice, read a variety of children's books aloud, well before your presentation, ensuring you embody the characters and the storyline. This is best done in the company of a child who can fully appreciate your efforts; however, reading it aloud to yourself will do the trick as well. Make your voice increase in speed and go higher in pitch if you read an exciting passage. Make it slow down and lower it an octave or two for scary or sad parts. Put space between words, punctuating the significance of each one when you want to place emphasize on a key message.

Don't have time for that?

Smile.

Smile while you speak. Those pearly whites instantly add personality to your voice and your overall countenance. The degree to which you speak with inflections is driven by your mood, and your facial expressions dictate your mood. A flat face with no expression leads to—you guessed it—a flat voice. Conversely, the energy from a smile will come through in your words, and your audience will thank you for it.

15. Refrain from reading.

Whether you speak with inflections and are animated or not, an audience truly prefers it if you do not read to them. Sure. There are those direct quotes that, if paraphrased, would not have the same effect. Definitely read those to your audience. However, resist the temptation to read your slides to your audience. First, the audience can silently read your slide faster than you can read it aloud to everyone.[5] Second, with only a few exceptions, a slide deck should contain no full sentences and should have no more than five to seven bullets per slide with a max of seven words per bullet.[6] Finally, try this strategy so you don't have to concern yourself with any of that: Create slides that are each filled with a high-resolution, eye-catching image or graphic and just a few words, if any words at all. The words or, better yet, the image itself with no words on the slide serves as a trigger, reminding you of what you plan to discuss. For instance, if you plan to discuss the ups and downs of the stock market, consider an image of a seesaw, then go into your spiel. It makes for a more memorable experience for your listeners.

16. Never diminish your power or presence.

For instance, avoid…

a. saying it is your first time, e.g., making a presentation, presenting on that topic, traveling out of the country, et cetera.

b. saying "I don't know."[7]

c. folding your arms; remain open and warm.[8]

17. Never say "I know I'm all over the place."

When you say this, you make it clear that you know you have let down your audience; you know you have not done the best job you can to facilitate a positive experience for your audience.

If you know you can be "all over the place" when facilitating a presentation, then be proactive; take a minute to craft an agenda or a quick list of headlines beforehand, and follow them. It does not have to be anything fancy or elaborate. You already know what you plan to cover, right? All you need are the three to five bullets you intend to discuss. Jot them down, then tell your listener(s) your agenda as you start or use your headlines throughout the presentation. This way, they are prepared for what's to come. The bonus here is not only does it help the audience easily follow your thoughts, but it also keeps you on track and makes you appear prepared and poised.

18. Never say "I'm sorry; I know that's a lot of information."

It negatively impacts your overall presentation performance in a number of ways.

First, the statement adds nothing of value to your presentation and calls attention to a lack of preparation. You should not have to offer up apologies if you planned and then delivered an exceptional experience, right?

Next, the statement does not make you or your presentation appear impressive. When someone says "I'm sorry; I know that's a lot of information," the speaker is not sincerely feeling apologetic for what he or she did. The fact is the presenter wants listeners to embrace the "a lot of information" part because the presenter thinks this flood of information makes him or her appear impressive and really knowledgeable. "I'm sorry; I know that's a lot of information" is code for "Wowee! Look at me! And look at how much I know!" But ... Newsflash! It is in no way remarkable (in a good way) to your audience.

Finally, no one wants "a lot of information," which equates to an information dump. Your audience does not want to drink from a firehose when you present. It wants to take manageable sips, receiving chunks of information at reasonable intervals with opportunities to think about what that information means and how they can use it. What your audience wants is an organized presentation of content that anyone can easily follow and remember long after your presentation has concluded.[9]

To fix it, first, stop saying "I'm sorry; I know that's a lot of information." Second, see number 17.

19. Never say "I know you can't see this slide." (This probably annoys me more than anything!)

There is absolutely no point whatsoever to include in your presentation a slide that your audience cannot read, see, or understand. It adds no value to your presentation.

There can be a number of reasons a slide is difficult to see. For instance, there could be too much information on a slide that has been squeezed on it by using a font that is entirely too small; there may be complicated graphs and charts, and the eyes do not know where to go. Or there may be an image that is of poor quality. To fix this, put in place best practices for slide design, which is covered in "The Only Presentation Plan You Will Ever Need Part 1: Behind the Scenes" in chapter 4.

If it's content that only you can decipher, then put it in your notes for your private reference, but do not share it with the audience if it's in a format that does not allow them to make sense of it. If it's information the audience needs, then ensure the slide is designed in a way everyone can read it.

20. Never introduce yourself by saying "For those of you who don't know me …."

Are you are suggesting everyone *should* know you? Is your intent to introduce yourself to only those who do *not* know you? And for those who *don't* know you, are you saying they're losers?

Listen. I know that's not what you're thinking when you say that; however, what in the world does that phrase mean—"For those of you who don't know me …"—and why use it in the first place?

Simply state "My name is _____." Period.

You are your brand, so it does not matter if people already know you or not; always announce yourself, and put in your name and your personal introduction the power they deserve.

> More on this is covered in *Show Up and Show Out: 52 Communication Habits to Make You Even More Unforgettable.*

21. Never let them see you sweat.

No matter if …

- you got lost while trying to find the place …

- technology fails …

- a slide is missing …

- your video does not play …

- your font does not correctly show …

- an activity seems to flop …

- you lose your train of thought …

- anything goes wrong …

SMILE, and make it clear that you've got this under control. There's nothing you cannot figure out or that you cannot get someone to help you figure out.

If you did not come with the intent of setting the audience on fire, then don't bother showing up. Seriously. Don't even get out of the bed. Show up to impress your audience, and equally as important, show up to impress yourself. Be able to walk away and say "Wow! I crushed that!"

---

[1]For more on microphones, see "Use a Mic. End of Story." in chapter 5.

[2]For a list of what to do before your presentation, see "The Only Presentation Plan You Will Ever Need Part 3: Your Quick and Clean Checklist" in chapter 4.

[3]For more on dealing with tech fails, see "How to Expertly Handle a Tech Fail" in chapter 5.

[4]For more on expertly dealing with missteps, see "What to Do if You Experience a Misstep in the Middle of Your Presentation" in chapter 5.

[5]For more on why you should never read your slides, see "It's Not Okay If You Read Your Slides to the Audience" in chapter 5.

[6]For help with slide design, see number 6 in "The Only Presentation Plan You Will Ever Need Part 1: Behind the Scenes" in chapter 4.

[7]For a more powerful alternative to answering questions to which you do not know the answer, see chart 1 in "Your Speech May Be a Victim of Wimpy Words" in chapter 1.

[8]To get ideas on what to do with your arms and hands, see "How to Use Nonverbal Communication to Silently Communicate Your Confidence" in chapter 1 or number 10, "Capitalize on Non-Verbal Language," of "The Only Presentation Plan You Will Ever Need: Part 2" in chapter 4.

[9]For more on how not to overwhelm your audiences, see "How to Prevent Information Overload" in chapter 3.

THE ULTIMATE PRESENTER MINDSET

There are those times when you are scheduled to make a presentation, but you simply do not feel up to it. Not at all. Not for a minute. So, what do you do? Do you phone it in? Cancel and reschedule? See if a replacement is available?

Here are real scenarios, most of which I have personally experienced, plus what the best presenters do even in the worst of times. It is tough, but this is the mindset to have no matter what.

Scenario 1: You fear presenting.

Perhaps it has been ages since you made a presentation, or the last time you made one, it totally flopped. Regardless, when you show up for a presentation, the last impression you want to give is one that suggests you are scared out of your wits or that you do not have your act together. Leave the audience with the impression that you are in utmost control. And that presentation that flopped? It is done and over. Stick a fork in it. You learned what worked and what did not pan out, and you have moved forward. Or what if it has been a long time since you presented? That is perfectly fine, too. Do not let the audience know it has been a significant amount of time since you last took to the stage. There's no need to proclaim "I'm so scared" or "It's been ages since I made a presentation!" Ask yourself "What point am I proving to anyone by uttering anything of the sorts?"

The Ultimate Mindset: Practice like it is the performance of a lifetime, then get out there and crush it.

Scenario 2: You and the audience are not gelling.

It is terrifying, but it happens. I remember many, many moons ago—maybe around 2011 or so—a colleague and I were delivering concurrent presentations in different parts of a building to groups of faculty members in California. During a break, I scurried over to the colleague and asked him if he was getting a weird vibe from the educators in his room. He was indeed. "Okay. Good." Not "good" as in I was glad he was getting the stink eye, too, but "good" as in I was glad I was not alone, that perhaps it was not 100 percent my fault that the audience was not loving everything I was saying.

We found out later that before our presentations, during the 8:00 a.m. plenary session, the faculty had been told there was a ton of new policies being put in place for the new term; they needed to enforce the policies and comply, as applicable; and raises for the new year were in jeopardy. "And with that, ladies and gentlemen, please go forth, and soak in everything the presenters have to give you!"

REALLY?!

The feelings I was sensing in my session were not personal. They were real. The audience had been slammed with all kinds of new information that required time to process, but instead, everyone was expected to immediately shift into gear and participate with full engagement and a happy face.

Yeah, right.

The Ultimate Mindset: Keep your game face on, do not worry about what you cannot control (e.g., audience attitudes), and give the crowd an unforgettable experience.

Scenario 3: You are so tired until you cannot think, walk, or talk straight.

Imagine presenting an afternoon webinar, zipping off to the airport, flying three hours to the east, hardly sleeping, presenting a two-hour in-person workshop the next morning, sprinting back to your hotel room after the workshop to moderate another webinar, then dashing off to the airport to fly to another city only to facilitate that in-person workshop again the next day. That sounds extreme and ridiculous, right? I have done it. (And this is a reality faced by many professional speakers out there!)

The Ultimate Mindset: You have two options. Either you tell everyone how tired you are (and even look and perform in a fatigued way) OR you show up, give it your all, and knock your audiences' socks off. After all, you can sleep another time (maybe even on the plane). For which type of performance do *you* want to be remembered?

Scenario 4: You receive devastating/world-rocking/ mind-blowing news just before a presentation.

Picture it. Early May 2018. San Diego, California. The convention center. (Yes, I am channeling my inner Sophia Petrillo from "The Golden Girls.") It was approximately 12:50 p.m. when I was on my way to the speaker ready room to make final tweaks to my slide deck in preparation to present at 3:00 p.m. Suddenly, I read a unique and incredibly familiar name on a conference-goer's name badge. There were 10,000+ people in attendance at this conference; the odds of me running into this person and then even engaging in a conversation with him were one in a billion—make that one in a trillion. I knew if I approached him, the experience would surely be rattling. However, I did not want to get on the plane back to Phoenix the next day, after hearing President Barack Obama speak—yeah, I am doing some name-dropping—wondering "what if " had I not chosen to approach him. I will not go into details here, but do know that the encounter and the huge secret that was revealed during the course of our conversation left us both totally shaken. Totally. In my mind, I was thinking "How in the world am I going to get through this presentation *now*?!" But I also had to tell myself "Suck it up, buttercup." I had a presentation in just over two hours; 400 to 500 people were going to be in the room, and cancelling or finding a replacement was just not an option. I showed up and did what I had to do. Period. That is the route you must take—recognizing it is not always appropriate to project your pain or struggles onto the audience. That is not what everyone came to see or hear. It is not that I'm suggesting you become a robot or that the audience would be unsympathetic to your plight; it is simply not their expectation that you will fall apart on stage or that the presentation will turn into an episode of "Dr. Phil."

The Ultimate Mindset: Give the audience that for which everyone came to see and hear, which is you giving them the fire! Try to keep it together as best you can for the duration of your presentation, then make a mad dash for the exit so you can find the privacy and space to process it all. Yes, your overall energy will be impacted as was mine, but again, how do you want to be remembered?

REAL TALK PRINCIPLE

Make yourself unforgettable for all the right reasons.

Scenario 5: You are making a presentation on what you know is your last day or one of your last days on the job.

This is a tough one, especially if you did not initiate the career change. And even if you did, there may be a feeling within you that makes you want to just dial it in, wrap it up, and call it a day. You cannot do this. When you are making a presentation, you are doing more than representing a company; you are representing yourself. You can tell everyone "This is my last day," but why do so if it has no bearing on the presentation and/or whether the audience will be taken care of after your departure from the company? Give a performance as if you are going to be in that position for the next 25 years, and leave no one the wiser. (And again, I have been here. Seattle... April 07, 2016... based on the performance I gave, you would have thought I was going to be selling the product on which I was presenting for the next five decades!) The degrees of separation are getting smaller and smaller. As such, you never know when paths will cross again. You do not want to be remembered as that person who made a presentation and obviously did not give a care.

The Ultimate Mindset: Always remember the bigger picture— your career, your reputation, your future, and your brand. It's not just a presentation; it's a representation of you. Press on, and make it sizzle!

REFLECT, REVIEW, AND RESPOND: DO YOU KNOW HOW TO ENSURE YOU ALWAYS SIZZLE?

1. How do you ensure you do not go over your allotted time when you present?

2. What is your strategy for when you will take questions during your presentations?

3. What do you do to ensure difficult audience members do not derail you?

4. What is your plan for answering any kind of question your audience poses to you?

5. How do you ensure you do not make the amateur move of reading your slides to your audience?

6. What particulars do you need to take into account when using a microphone? In what instances, if ever, can you forego using a mic?

7. Will you stand on a podium or stage or not? Will you stand at a lectern or not? Are there certain times during your presentation when you will do one or the other? If so, then when?

8. How do you handle a technology glitch?

9. What does it mean if someone leaves your presentation, and what, if anything, should you do as a result?

10. If you have to present boring information or the same content several times, then what can you do to make it more interesting for both you and your audience?

11. What should you keep in mind when presenting to an international audience?

12. What are at least five common mistakes presenters make? How are they fixed or avoided altogether?

13. What is the ultimate mindset you need to have as a presenter? For what do you want to be remembered after you make a presentation?

ABOUT THE AUTHOR

Have you ever experienced an energy that made you move to the edge of your seat or that had you stand to your feet? What about an excitement that stayed with you and had you talking about it long after an event ended? That is the best way to describe Bridgett McGowen, an award-winning author, an award-winning publisher, and an award-winning international professional speaker who is known to be both comical and memorable. She will not only energize you but will inspire you to not let anyone or anything get in the way of you being the most unforgettable person in the room.

Bridgett has been a professional speaker since 2001 and has spoken on programs alongside prominent figures such as former President Barack Obama, Deepak Chopra, Alex Rodriguez (A-Rod), Oprah Winfrey, Shonda Rhimes, Katie Couric, Janelle Monae, Sir Richard Branson, Indra Nooyi, Stacey Abrams, Dr. Mae Jemison, Common, Amy Cuddy, Sara Blakely, Issa Rae, and Mel Robbins.

The prestigious University of Texas at Austin presented her with a Master Presenter Award; Canada-based One Woman has presented her with two Fearless Woman Awards; and she has facilitated hundreds of workshops, keynote and commencement addresses, conference sessions, trainings, and webinars to thousands of students and professionals who are positioned all around the globe.

Bridgett's expertise and presentations have been sought after by companies, post-secondary institutions, and organizations such as Centers for Disease Control and Prevention (CDC), Fifth Third Bank, Vanguard Investments, LifeLock, Symantec, Kentucky Fried Chicken, McGraw-Hill Education, LinkedIn Local, Association for Talent Development, Chegg, CenterPoint Energy, New York University (NYU), Doña Ana Community College, National Association of Women Sales Professionals, Independence University, Turnitin, National Association of Black Accountants, Miller-Motte College, Prairie View A&M University, and Society for Human Resource Management (SHRM). She has been quoted by Transizion, has contributed to UpJourney, and has appeared as a guest on multiple podcasts as well as Phoenix Business Radio to showcase her expertise in the professional speaking industry.

Bridgett has also taught for Prairie View A&M University, which is a part of the Texas A&M University System; Lone Star College System; and University of Phoenix. From 2009 until 2016, while in the employ of an educational technology company, she traveled the country researching, designing, and facilitating faculty and professional development workshops and webinars for dozens of universities as well as community, career, and technical colleges. She has earned a Bachelor of Arts, cum laude in Communication and a Master of Arts, summa cum laude; is a member of Alpha Kappa Alpha Sorority, Incorporated; is a member of the International Society of Female Professionals; and has been featured by CBS, NBC, and Fox Media.

Bridgett is also an Entrepreneur Leadership Network Writer, a former Forbes Coaches Council contributor, a *Medium* contributor, a *Thrive Global* contributor, and has been published in the Association for Talent Development's *TD* magazine. She is the author of several books to include *Show Up and Show Out: 52 Communication Habits to Make You Even More Unforgettable*; *Own the Microphone*, an amazing collaboration with 50 professional speakers from around the globe; *Rise and Sizzle: Daily Communication and Presentation Strategies for Sales, Business, and Higher Ed Pros*; and two editions of *REAL TALK: What Other Experts Won't Tell You About How to Make Presentations That Sizzle* with the first edition winning the 2020 Best Indie Book Award in the non-fiction business and communication category and claiming the title of being a 2020 Next Generation Indie Book Award Finalist. Bridgett is also the host of the highly rated *Own the Microphone* podcast and the owner of the award-winning independent publishing company, BMcTALKS Press.

Bridgett's mission now is to help as many professionals as possible move away from being ordinary and flying under the radar, to dig deep and give the people the best versions of themselves even when they don't feel like it, to not let anything or anyone get in their way of being the most unforgettable person in the room. Bridgett lives with her family in the Phoenix, Arizona area, and she absolutely loves beautiful sunsets.

CPSIA information can be obtained
at www.ICGtesting.com
Printed in the USA
BVHW091023260922
647807BV00001B/46